June, 1972

Michelangelo

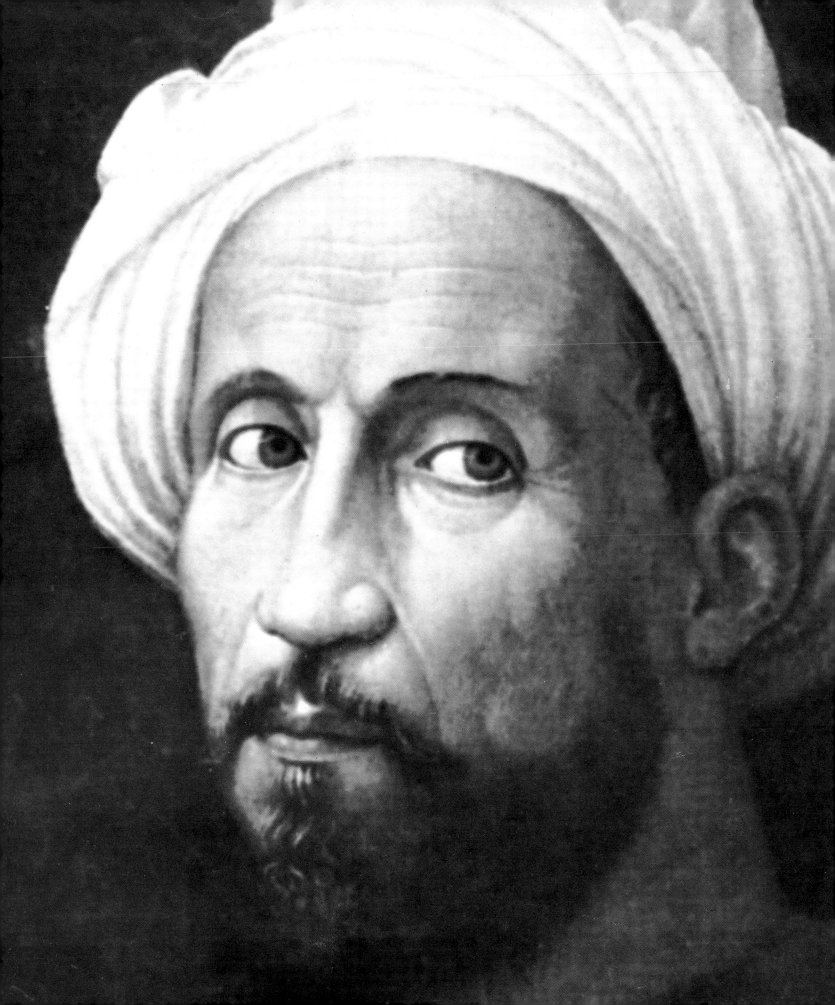

Nicholas Wadley

Michelangelo

The Colour Library of Art

Hamlyn

London · New York · Sydney · Toronto

Acknowledgments

The paintings and objects in this volume are reproduced by kind permission of the following collectors and galleries to which they belong: By gracious permission of Her Majesty the Queen (figures 8, 9); Albertina, Vienna (figure 2); Ashmolean Museum, Oxford (plate 53); Biblioteca Apostolica Vaticana (figure 7); The Trustees of the British Museum, London (signature on cover); The Earl of Leicester, Holkham Hall (figure 1); Metropolitan Museum of Art, New York, Purchase 1924, Joseph Pulitzer Bequest (plate 16); Musée du Louvre, Paris (plate 24); The President and Council, Royal Academy of Arts, London (plate 7); Count Seilern, London (figure 10). Uffizi Gallery, Florence (plate 6).

The figures and plates were taken by the following photographers: Mansell-Alinari, Florence (figure 5); E. Boudot-Lamotte, Paris (plate 48); Wallace Heaton Ltd, London (figure 8); Michael Holford, London (figures 3, 4, 6, plates 24, 53); Denis Hughes-Gilbey, London (plate 7); Bruno del Priore, Rome (plates 10-15, 17, 18, 20, 21, 38, 40, 43, 44); Scala Florence (plates 1-6, 8, 9, 19, 22, 23, 25-37, 41, 45-47, 49, 50-52); George Spearman Ltd, Windsor (figure 9).

The publishers gratefully acknowledge the copyright owners' permission to reproduce and quote from the following works: Bruno M. Appollonj Ghetti, Opere Architettoniche di Michelangelo a Firenze (Monumenti Italian II), Libreria dello Stato, Rome (figures 3, 4, 6); on page 26, Charles Holroyd, Michelangelo Buonarroti, Duckworth, London, 1903, 1911; Elizabeth Gilmore Holt, A Documentary History of Art (Vol. II), Doubleday and Co., New York, © Princeton University Press, 1947, 1958; Ludwig Goldscheider, Michelangelo, Phaidon, London, 1959; E. H. Ramsden, The Letters of Michelangelo, Peter Owen, London, © E. H. Ramsden 1963; Giorgio Vasari, The Lives of the Most Eminent Painters, Sculptors and Architects (Vol. IX), translated by Gaston du C. de Vere, The Medici Society, London, © Random House Inc., 1959.

Contents

Published by
THE HAMLYN PUBLISHING GROUP LIMITED
London · New York · Sydney · Toronto
Hamlyn House, Feltham, Middlesex, England

© copyright Paul Hamlyn Limited 1965
First published in this edition 1969
Reprinted 1971

ISBN 0 600 03784 3

Printed in Italy by Officine Grafiche Arnoldo Mondadori, Verona

THE PLATES

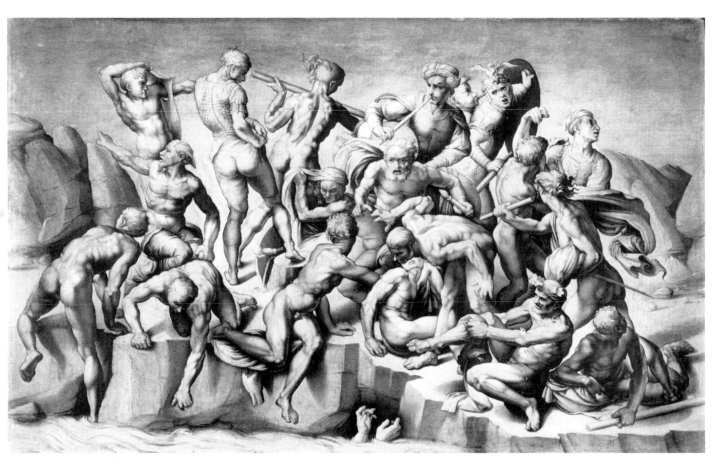

1 Sangallo: Copy of Michelangelo's *Battle of Cascina*

Introduction

We have been admirers of the great Michelangelo many years now, since the fame of his genius depends no less on the peerless skill of his sculpture than on the unique and illustrious craftsmanship of his painting, and we ourselves have seen his works in various places and feel that no praise can ever be enough for them. Wherefore, we would wish to bestow a favour upon him . . . we charge you to arrange that you meet him and tell him how highly we regard him and how kindly we are disposed towards him. Then ask him, on our behalf, as seems to you most effective and endearing, to be pleased to do us this honour, and agree to give us the pleasure of anything from his own hand, either a sculpture or a painting, as he thinks fit. We do not prefer one to the other, just so long as it is from his own hand . . . This is our one especial and cherished wish. We have no thought of one material rather than another; nor is one subject dearer to us than another; we only desire to have a work of his great genius . . . if he has nothing ready that he thinks we would be happy to have, ask him if he would at least let us have some drawing from his hand—even a charcoal drawing—so that in this way we can assuage our burning desire, our most heartfelt wish, until he can send us something finished. Let this be made as he wills, a statue or a painting. We are certain it can only give us the deepest delight . . . Never shall we forget so great a joy.

The ingratiating tone of this plea, written in 1527 by the Marquis of Mantua to his Florentine agent, is not untypical of the attitude of Michelangelo's innumerable prospective patrons. Like many others, it was doomed to disappointment (even though the campaign persisted in this vein for eleven years).

Although it often proved a considerable disadvantage to him, the extraordinary nature and power of Michelangelo's art was recognised by his contemporaries. The fact that Vasari not only made Michelangelo's work the climax of his three-volumed history of art, but also published a separate biography of him in 1568, is more than a token of personal esteem. In confidently prophesying that 'it is impossible that we shall ever see anything better', Vasari was voicing the opinion of his time. To his contemporaries Michelangelo was the supreme example of a new kind of artist: an artist of divine genius, owing no obligation to a master, respected by rather than respecting his patrons and for whom art was a compulsive inner calling rather than a profession. The inevitable comparisons that we draw between him and his two fellow-giants of the High Renaissance, Leonardo and Raphael (both of whom he outlived by over forty years), only serve to emphasise Michelangelo's uniqueness. Leonardo, the multi-minded 'universal man', emphasises the single-minded determination with which Michelangelo saw painting, sculpture and architecture as one art involving the same prob-

lems; Raphael, the superbly gifted public performer, whose facile talent could be turned, with the assistance of a large and smoothly run workshop, to meet any commission that arose, emphasises Michelangelo's increasingly introverted struggle for the realisation of his ideas—a struggle that was waged against demanding patrons, inadequate assistants and above all against the terrifying standards of his own ideals. Raphael's lucid, harmonious, Classical art became a copybook ideal for a succession of academies. Michelangelo's art was too personal to be successfully shared in any stylistic sense. Without the authority of his personality behind them, his characteristic forms, poses and gestures appear false and theatrical in the work of followers and copyists. From the start the themes which he treated and the means with which he treated them were relatively limited; it is the way in which he stretched these limited means almost to breaking point that explains his profound liberating influence. The artists who gained most from his work were those who, like Rubens and Bernini, could see that his greatness lay beyond his style and his personal mannerisms.

For a native of fifteenth-century Florence, Michelangelo's early artistic career was exceptional in two important respects. It was customary for great emphasis to be laid on draughtsmanship and customary to study the antique and the great Florentine masters. But not only did Michelangelo make an unfashionable choice in the artists he admired (Giotto, Masaccio and Donatello, rather than contemporary masters such as Botticelli, Ghirlandaio and Pollaiuolo), he also adopted an attitude towards these early sources which was distinctly original. He rejected an art of great sophistication and refinement for an art which was at once monumental and intensely expressive and in doing so seems to have been instinctively seeking those qualities which were to constitute the personality of his mature style. The vigorously hatched—almost chiselled—drawings made from Masaccio's monumental figure paintings isolate and emphasise their structural mass and expressive force, and the *Madonna of the Stairs* relief (plate 1), full of Donatello's spatial subtlety and of his bitter-sweet melancholy, already shows that innate sense of scale and weight that found its final expression in the architecture of St Peter's.

His debts to his masters, the painter Ghirlandaio and the sculptor Bertoldo, seem on the evidence of his work to have lain chiefly in acquiring technical proficiency. Michelangelo was a student in the Medici sculpture school (supervised by Bertoldo) when his outstanding ability and intelligence were noticed by Lorenzo de' Medici ('the Magnificent') who took him into the Medici household almost as a member of the family. The most significant formative influences on the spiritual character of his art came first from the Neoplatonist circles of the Medici house and secondly from the sermons of Savonarola. The programme of the humanist philosophers was a search for the understanding of the fundamental ethics and principles of human morality and behaviour both spiritual and physical: their research was based extensively on Plato's rediscovered works and was essentially an attempt to rationalise, praising intellectual mastery and calling sensual emotions and impressions into question.

Savonarola's preaching in Florence in the 1490s was openly opposed to the material wealth of the Medici court and the popular success of his ascetic, anti-materialistic sermons was largely responsible for its downfall. He was the guiding light of the new republic of 1494, organising public 'bonfires of vanities' and championing its stern rejection of all excesses and indulgences. Papal disapproval of him culminated in his excommunication (1497) and his public burning for heresy and sedition (1498), but the intensity of his pessimistic prophecies of doom was not easily forgotten during later troubles such as the Sack of Rome (1527).

Both influences encouraged in Michelangelo a disregard of superficial appearances and a deep involvement with the spiritual essence underlying the surface of reality, already clearly evident in the brooding silence of the *Madonna of the Stairs*. The conflict between these two views of life—one an optimistic, pagan rationalism, the other a rather pessimistic yearning after Christian purity—although largely reconciled in mature works like the Sistine Ceiling or the Medici Chapel, was the main cause of his later mental anguish and hence of the emotionally disturbed character of his late paintings, sculpture and sonnets.

Lorenzo the Magnificent died in 1492 and without his leadership the Medici family quickly—and justifiably—fell from favour. In 1494 the Medici house was expelled from Florence. Michelangelo, an intimate member of the household, anticipated the crisis and left the city, fleeing first to Bologna and Venice and then, in 1496, to Rome. When he returned to Florence in 1501 it was in triumph, as a master in his own right.

Two works executed in Rome were responsible for this reputation: the overlifesize *Bacchus* (plate 2), an unsteady youth with glazed eyes and open mouth, and his first *Pietà*. Although the *Bacchus* was admired for its prodigious technical accomplishment, it is traditionally the least liked of Michelangelo's sculptures, the subtle interpretation of the subject being considered at times repellent, at others simply excessively anti-Classical. The St Peter's *Pietà* (plate 3) however, was immediately recognised for what it is: a milestone in Italian sculpture.

It is the first sculpture of the High Renaissance, that brief climax of Classical perfection after the fifteenth century's struggle for knowledge and mastery. The whole idea of the *Pietà* (almost unprecedented in Italy) is typical of that climax in its concentration and simplification. The complete range of feeling associated with Christ's passion is condensed into two eloquently simple figures. The Virgin, still a tender young mother, nurses the limp body of the crucified Christ, grown to early manhood but seeming pathetically small, in a poignant echo of his infancy. A veil of gentle sorrow is decorously drawn across the emotional intensity of the subject without wholly negating it. Michelangelo's ability to express subtle shades of human emotion rivals the contemporary work of Leonardo's maturity. It is here heightened by the matchless finish of the polished marble, investing the image with an aura of unapproachable fragility and perfection. The almost precious beauty and sensitivity of this work are unique in Michelangelo's oeuvre: nowhere else are the sentiments so gently handled or the forms so exquisitely finished. But it was undoubtedly these qualities which overwhelmed his contemporaries and accounted for his successful return to Florence as a famous sculptor, to be greeted by a burst of commissions, both public and private.

For the next four years all went well. Important commissions, his ambition and his prodigious ability were perfectly matched and this happy situation produced a group of works which were a fitting culmination to the Florentine Renaissance.

The colossal *David* (plate 4) is both a climax to the Renaissance tradition of the heroic youth and an overture to Michelangelo's lifelong preoccupation with the male nude as a vehicle of artistic expression. Technically it is the second great masterpiece of his early years: his achievement in carving the figure from a single partly mutilated block of marble was in itself deeply admired by contemporaries. Stylistically it is the final statement

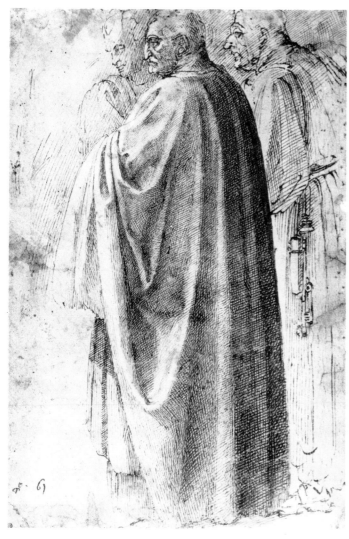

2 Michelangelo's copy of *Three Standing Figures* by Masaccio

of his Classical period, reconciling mastery of his means with a controlled rationalisation of subject matter. The sixteen-foot nude figure is handled with complete anatomical authority and the fluent ease of the pose shows Michelangelo's mastery of the Classical idiom. But the Classical ideal is—as in the *Bacchus*—blended with a very powerful sense of the individual. The lack of tension expressed by the easily hanging right arm and the relaxed left leg is complemented by the agitated slightly large hands and by the exaggerated twist of the head with its knotted hair, creased brow, and alert, serious eyes. The traditional Classical *contrapposto** is injected with an expressive restlessness

*A type of pose dating back to antiquity, in which the parts of the body are counterposed around an implied central axis: usually there is a balance between the upper half of the body turned to face in one direction and the lower half in the other direction.

and a sense of potential action and muscular energy which is only momentarily dormant.

The *David* originally stood (like its replica today) outside the Palazzo Vecchio, the Florentine town hall, as an alert guardian of the Christian faith and of just government. Like Donatello's *St George*, to which it is a High Renaissance counterpart, it was a symbol of Florence's collective virility. But even at this, his most rational period, Michelangelo's work was not wholly identifiable with the High Renaissance spirit. It is without the sweet idealism of Leonardo, the graceful charm of Raphael or the serenely balanced harmony of Bramante. *David* leaves one disturbed by a dynamic presence rather than with satisfied senses. What above all else did identify Michelangelo as the supreme High Renaissance artist was his natural ability. Gifted, it seemed to his contemporaries, to a superhuman degree, he resolved with ease and on a monumental scale ideas that had been struggled with by artists right through the previous century. Three circular panels or *tondi*, one painted and two carved, that he carried out for private patrons during these years—1503–6—illustrate the selective simplicity and strength of his solutions.

Michelangelo later defined his attitude to painting as believing that 'painting and sculpture are one and the same thing', but with this qualification: 'painting should be considered excellent as it approaches the effect of relief, while relief should be considered bad in proportion as it approaches the effect of painting'. At this time he was solely preoccupied with the sculptor's problems and the *Doni Tondo* (plate 6), his earliest known painting, is strictly an exploration of three-dimensional form through the illusionistic medium of paint. The *Holy Family* is another typically 'condensed' subject. The figures are welded into a monumental sculptural block isolated by colour and definition from the apse-like background. The significant forms are stressed by contrasts of light and dark, just as, in the Royal Academy relief (plate 7), they are stressed by the projection and recession of the carved surface. The uniformity of the tight, wiry contour that contains the painted group even suggests that, like a relief, the group is not fully in the round but flat and smooth at the back. The relief was a form which lay at the heart of his whole conception of sculpture and although these two *tondi* (the other is in the Bargello, Florence) were the last he made, the idea of the relief lies behind much of his later work and is also fundamental to his approach to fresco painting and to architecture.

By 1504 the *David* was completed and the triumph of its universal acclaim was rewarded with two major public commissions in Florence. The first was for a painting to decorate one of the long walls of the Great Council Hall in the Palazzo Vecchio: this was to be a companion piece to a painting already commissioned for an adjacent wall space from Leonardo. The second was for twelve larger-than-lifesize statues of the Apostles for the nave of the Cathedral. The horizons must have seemed limitless. At the age of 29 Michelangelo was given a sculpture contract of almost unprecedented scale with full confidence that he could produce the figures at the rate of one per year; and on the other hand he was ranked as a painter side by side with Leonardo, the 52-year-old master—and what a confrontation that might have been had either painting been completed. He started work on the cartoon for the painting and ordered marble for the first six Apostles, but before either project could get any further the situation was suddenly (and permanently) transformed. In the spring of 1505 he was summoned to Rome by the energetic new Pope, Julius II, to design his tomb.

During the 1500s Rome was quickly replacing Florence as the most important centre of artistic activity in Italy. Julius II, as a part of his relentless campaign to restore papal authority and make Rome once more into an imperial capital, was responsible for large-scale patronage of all the arts (a patronage which in some ways made the High Renaissance possible). The task of making a memorial tomb for this 'Pope-Emperor' was sufficiently challenging to Michelangelo's imagination to compensate for the distraction from his work in Florence. The project quickly absorbed all of his energies: its fulfilment was to be his most cherished dream and—in the event—his most bitter frustration. Plans were submitted and approved for a free-standing mausoleum which contained the sarcophagus inside and was decorated outside with over forty marble figures and four bronze reliefs. It was to be a tomb without parallel even in antiquity and Michelangelo probably offered to redesign the apse of St Peter's as a site for it. He spent eight months selecting suitable marble at Carrara and returned to find that the Pope—preoccupied by now with his plans for the building of a new St Peter's by Bramante—was not prepared to advance any more money for the tomb and refused even to see him.

Incensed, Michelangelo returned to his work in Florence and it is not over-romantic to sense something of his frustration, mistrust and anger in the unfinished *St Matthew* (plate 8). The only one of the twelve apostles for the cathedral which he started, it has a new sense of writhing energy that is fundamentally anti-Classical. The revolutionary pose of the saint, dynamic and outspokenly expressive, is matched by the undisciplined urgency of the carving. These qualities (although presumably diminished through our third-hand knowledge) were also present in the *Battle of Cascina* (figure 1), Michelangelo's cartoon for the Palazzo Vecchio painting. This drawing served as a model for all young Florentine artists from its completion in 1506 to its destruction in 1516: Cellini called it 'the school of the world'. What excited this admiration was the virtuoso display of anatomical knowledge and the extent to which the nude could be made the sole means of artistic expression. Michelangelo chose to represent not the battle itself but the moment of psychological crisis when the unexpected approach of the enemy was announced. A sudden tumultuous energy runs through the group, subjecting the human body to a succession of expressive, gesticulating postures. The swift play of bodies and limbs and the coarse texture of flexed muscles express the sudden alarm of the bathing soldiers.

In the *St Matthew* this is taken further. The spiritual tensions expressed by the body's outward appearance have taken control, and the surface accuracy of the *David* or the tightly knotted muscles of the bathers have given way to a convulsive, stormy eruption of inner forces as the massive forms appear to churn about within the stone block. The change which evolved through these two works from his masterful Classicism, where outward appearance was perfected, to an inward visionary art where formal control was sacrificed to intensity of expression, has been attributed in part to the influence of the late antique sculpture of *Laocoön and his two sons*, discovered in Rome in 1506. The hysterical turbulence of the *Laocoön* must have moved him deeply and there is little doubt that its character encouraged his post-Classical development. But the change is also an expression of the disturbed stability of the artist's working environment. The perfect balance between his need to express and his opportunity to express that produced his early masterpieces no longer existed. From this point on he was increasingly driven by an urgent need to express *despite* the opportunities, which

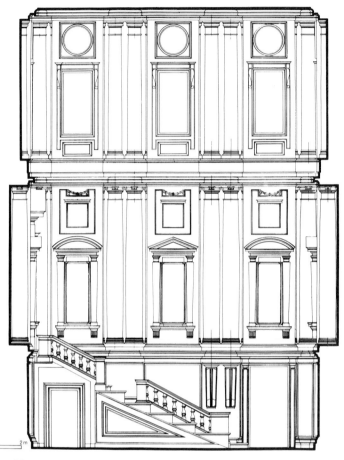

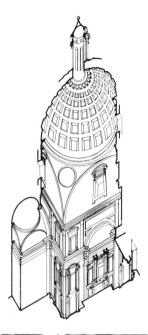

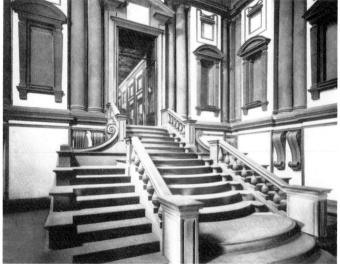

6 Isometric projection of the
   Medici Chapel

3 Elevation of the side wall of the Vestibule, Biblioteca Laurenziana, San
   Lorenzo, Florence

5 The Vestibule staircase, Biblioteca Laurenziana, San Lorenzo, Florence

4 Plan and section of the Reading Room
   and Vestibule, Biblioteca Laurenziana,
   San Lorenzo, Florence

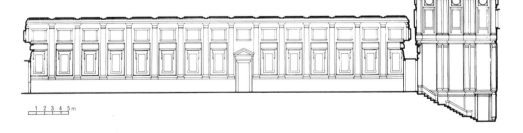

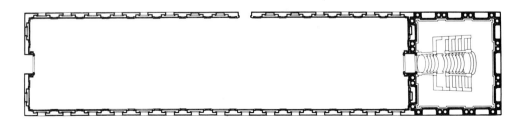

reached a climax in the emotional intensity of his last works.

The background to the great projects of his maturity is a distressing story of conflicting pressures and practical difficulties. In addition, they were all undertaken with the Julius Tomb project at least at the back of his mind. The commission in 1508 to decorate the vaults of the Sistine Chapel in Rome (plates 9–21) was accepted with reluctance. After a reconciliation with the Pope in Bologna (1506), this new project meant not only a fresh distraction from the Tomb, but also a total distraction from his work as a sculptor. He ostentatiously signed letters at this period 'Michelagniolo, scultore' and in fact his solution to the problem of vault decoration—neither wholly illusionistic nor wholly decorative—was essentially a sculptural one. He was inspired by the vault itself to construct a scheme which echoes and extends its actual structure and shape. The weight of the enthroned prophets and sibyls acts as a series of buttresses holding down the vault at the point at which it springs away from the wall, and the flatly curved surface of the barrel vault itself is emphasised by the painted stone bands which run across the ceiling dividing the nine history paintings. The scheme is like a massive relief which is at its highest point with the prophets and sibyls, decreasing in scale and projection through the nude athletes (ignudi) to the histories which are quite clearly painted on the flat ceiling surface, with no intention of illusionism, like canvases behind the stone frames.

The ceiling decoration is in no sense a co-ordinated trompe-l'oeil illusion. Although each one of the prophets and sibyls, considered in isolation, is painted in an illustionistc perspective scheme to be read from a fixed viewpoint on the chapel floor, these schemes when considered together contradict one another. Similarly the pairs of ignudi seated above the thrones are conceived from a separate series of fixed viewpoints which 'bend' the illusion forward towards the centre of the ceiling. Michelangelo's intention was not to create a technically perfect illusion, but to create an architectural framework which, while related to its context, was governed by its own immeasurable logic and structural forces. So while each individual part can in turn be studied and understood by the spectator, it is at the same time part of a total vision which defies understanding. This supernatural architectonic edifice which floats above the chapel is inhabited by a race of superhuman beings.

The formal unity of the paintings reflects the unity of the subject matter. The central theme of salvation represents Michelangelo's first comprehensive attempt to reconcile Neo-platonic philosophy with Christian beliefs and, like the *St Matthew*, shows his growing concern with a spiritual life underlying physical appearances. The nine history paintings, alternating in size, represent a dramatic sequence of three stories from the book of Genesis: starting from the altar end, the Creation, the story of Adam and the story of Noah. The central panel is the *Creation of Eve*, the turning point between the divine authority of God's creative acts and the final degradation of man in Noah's drunken stupor. To the spectator entering the chapel by the main door these histories are in reverse order (the order in which Michelangelo painted them). It is in this order that he intended them to be seen, as a progression from the servitude of the body to the liberation and uplifting of the soul. Amid the desolation of the *Deluge* (plate 11) man is caught in violent, ineffectual action, panic-stricken and at the mercy of circumstance. In the *Fall of Man* he is capable of decisive action, but the clumsy grabbing gesture of the sensuous Adam expresses the weakness of the flesh uncontrolled by the spirit. By contrast the Adam of the *Creation* expresses in his superhuman grace and perfection the supremacy of the spirit: the body at ease but the face burning with an inner intensity inspired by the closeness of the Creator. In the final 'earlier' scenes this intensity is completely released in the monumental, increasingly violent images of God. Here the soul achieves liberation, unimpaired by the presence of the human body. This main theme is supported throughout the decoration. The *ignudi* are an ideal human manifestation of heavenly perfection. The prophets and pagan sibyls, seekers after truth, build up in the degree of their contemplation and enlightenment to reach a climax in the figure of *Jonah* over the altar. The archetype of Christ through his miraculous salvation, he alone looks up to the figure of the Almighty overhead, representing a final moment of revelation. At this point Michelangelo's two schemes—the illusionistic and the pictorial—unite. The four corner spandrels represent scenes of miraculous salvation from the Old Testament and the lunettes depict the ancestors of Christ (descendants of Noah) as the humblest form of life in the ceiling's hierarchy, preoccupied only with day-to-day existence.

The extraordinary complexity of the ceiling's programme and the mastery of its organisation (in which, as far as we can gather, there was no intervention by the Pope or his advisers) are apt to overwhelm us into ignoring its outstanding innovation. In the *Battle of Cascina* cartoon (figure 1), Michelangelo revealed his intention to compose a fairly large wall fresco entirely with the human body: here this intention is carried through on a gigantic scale and the entire planned area (nearly 6,000 square feet) is conceived solely in terms of the figure. All of the Renaissance achievement in the rendering of rich stuffs and drapery and the fifteenth century's intensive study of the landscape both in detail and in atmospheric unity is forgone—look at the minimal stage properties of the *Expulsion* (plate 12), or the *Creation of Man* (plate 13). The bareness of setting is a deliberate foil for the lithe animation of the figures: as well as by its architectonic structure, the ceiling is unified by the sinewed web of its living population.

Contemporary critics such as Ludovico Dolce saw Michelangelo's concentrated use of the male nude as a limitation, compared for example with Raphael's 'mastery in every field'. But his intimate knowledge of this limited field enabled Michelangelo to achieve an extraordinarily wide range of expression: facial expression and rhetorical gesture are less important than the inflexions of stomach muscles, the shape of a thigh or the hang of a wrist. The personality and mood of his images are built out of these characteristics rather than from symbolic attributes. The discovery of expressiveness in an elongated limb or a muscular torso by the Florentine mannerists was a by-product of Michelangelo's 'limitation'. The nude body remained throughout his life his sole artistic means whether in terms of sublime idealisation or desolated imperfection. Our total picture of his art comprises an accumulation of impressions of the human physique subject to a multitude of different conditions. The nude needed no specific context in his subject matter: the object of painting and sculpture. he said, 'is to make figures', and he treated architectural members comparably as limbs and features related to a body. One need look no further than this to explain or justify the background figures of the *Doni Tondo* (plate 6) or the *ignudi* of the ceiling.

The first half of the ceiling (up to and including the *Creation of Eve*) was unveiled at the Pope's insistence in August 1511, and the rest in October 1512. The change between the two sections are modifications made by Michelangelo after seeing the first half in its entirety for the first time in 1511. The remainder was painted more quickly and conceived more as a whole. The figures are more dominant in scale, weight, colour and animation (the *ignudi*, prophets and sibyls as well as those in the Creation scenes). He eliminated the use of gold and silver and suppressed finish and detail in favour of a massive tonal unity. The whole scheme is held together by a powerful network of diagonal forces. The ceiling confirmed the development of his art from the High Renaissance to a dynamic, empirical, personal way of working. Where in the High Renaissance—or anywhere else, for that matter—would one expect to recognise the Almighty by the soles of His feet?

Unique in being his only major project to be completed in his lifetime, the Sistine Ceiling absorbed Michelangelo spiritually and physically for four years, to the exclusion of all other works and of almost any social contact. Its comprehensive character, combining aspects of sculpture and architecture in painting, is a turning point. Although remaining essentially a sculptor he now admitted to himself that the three arts were alternative means of expression with the same underlying principles. The great undertakings of his maturity (he worked on several simultaneously) were partially if not wholly architectural projects. At a unique moment in the history of art, his treatment of the three media had a complete sense of identity, all subjected to his expressive handling of plastic values.

The project for the Julius II Tomb was from the start a fusion of sculpture and architecture. The scale of Michelangelo's initial design was, while within the capability of his vision and his technique, given time, quite impracticable for an artist as much in demand as he was and—more important—for an artist as loath to delegate to others the task of realising his own conceptions. With each of the four revised contracts (1513, 1516, 1532, 1542) the tomb shrank in scale and ambition. By the 1520s it was so altered that Michelangelo had lost interest and enthusiasm, wishing only to fulfil his obligation as quickly as possible and so end the intolerably drawn out tragedy that his dream had become.

The tomb stands now (plate 22) as it was erected in 1545 in San Pietro in Vincoli, not even in St Peter's. It is a shallow wall tomb, thoroughly inconsistent in quality, scale, style and vision. Not only is the severe, monumental *Moses* (carved 1513–16; plate 23) uncomfortable in the company of the assistants' sterile work overhead, he is totally incompatible with the melting, visionary quality of Michelangelo's late style in the figures of *Rachel* and *Leah* on each side of him. The dream of a vast unified project which the tomb had represented for him from the first was never realised: we can only approach a sense of it from the other mature works that stemmed from the same ambition. His schemes for the three commissions in the Medici Church of San Lorenzo in Florence, which kept him from working on the tomb in the 1520s and 30s, were all related to the same central idea. They were for the church façade, a memorial chapel and a library to house the Medici collection. The façade of the church, conceived as a three-storey block, one bay deep and carrying a wealth of carved figures and reliefs, was abandoned, unstarted, in 1520. The Medici Chapel (plates 27–37) is far from complete. The two existing tombs are unfinished and neither the principal tomb nor the projected frescoes were even started. The chapel nevertheless offers a fuller insight than anything else into Michelangelo's ambition to unite sculpture and architecture into an expressive whole.

The first thing that one notices about the chapel is the strangely animated character of the architecture with its subtle, muted colour. The eight small doorways are crushed beneath heavy tabernacle niches overhead. The niches themselves are uncomfortably close together, squashing the Corinthian capitals into the corner between them. The capitals seem knotted in a third larger tomb designed for the wall facing the altar. So the curving lines of the dome overhead would have been echoed by these colossal shapes spreading out from the wall on to the floor: the naked inanimate cube of the building transformed into an organic sphere. One can only imagine how disturbing it might have been to stand within this inhabited, living setting. In fact the spectator was not intended to stand *in* it. The altar in the recessed sanctuary is turned about so that it faces out into the chapel and the kneeling worshipper in the sanctuary was to look beyond it into the space of the chapel, as if from the outside. It is like a three-dimensional altarpiece, a unique concept, to be experienced and meditated upon as a totality.

The exact subject matter of what was to be meditated upon has been the topic of much discussion: the main obstacles to solving the problem are the incompleteness of the chapel and, coupled with it, the knowledge that Michelangelo constantly changed his ideas while working on a project, improvising freely in both form and subject. It is difficult to go much further than our near certainty that he was once again concerned with the frenzied attempt to force their way out. This energy is diverted upwards, and overhead it swings out in the slow curves of the linear grey articulation through great flat areas of white plaster. The open airy rhythms of the upper two storeys reach a climax in the dome, a very original refinement upon that of the Pantheon, whose shallow coffers close upwards to the eye of the lantern, bringing the whole living structure to a serene conclusion.

The tombs of Giuliano and Lorenzo de' Medici (plates 29 and 30), facing each other from the side walls, provide a concentration in colour and sculptural richness as well as in subject matter. The niches behind the idealised seated portraits are the deepest points of recession in the walls and the tombs build up and back to them in a pyramid. This pyramid would have been strengthened by the large recumbent figures of River Gods which Michelangelo intended should lie in front of each tomb out on the chapel floor. The same would have applied to the fundamental significance of man's being and salvation, of his inner spiritual existence and his outward physical activity. These last conflicting aspects of man are opposed in the two tombs. *Giuliano de' Medici* (plates 29 and 31), a descendant of the marble *David*, sits alert and alive, his muscular torso flexed, his legs tensed, his head sharply turned. *Lorenzo* (plates 30 and 32) is physically inert like *Jeremiah* on the Sistine ceiling (plate 17), his hands nervous and awkward, his legs twisted together, his muscles loose and his face—a negative climax—lost in the shadow of the grotesque helmet-mask. This opposition of the active and the contemplative is restated in the respective pairs of allegorical figures reclining on the sarcophagi. The pair below Giuliano are totally contrasted in finish and in subject. *Night* (plate 33), highly polished, is a withered spent image, her body sagging and loose, while the monumental *Day* (plate 35), scarcely realised from the block, has a massive power. Angularly composed, they are opposite extremes in subject, symbols of physical exhaustion and strength. *Evening* and *Dawn* (plates 34 and 36), the intermediate, less positive, phases of the cycle, are more alike in their languid open poses and are both filled with an inner malaise, symbols of spiritual decline and reawakening. Similar themes were incorporated in most stages of the Julius Tomb project, and seem to have been carried over into the

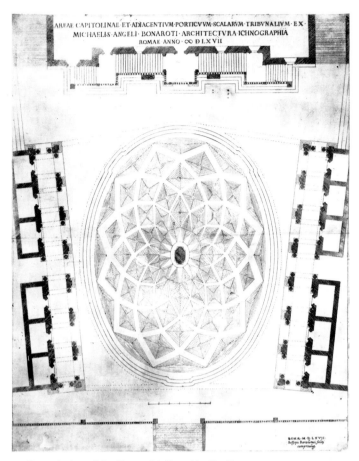

Ground plan of the Piazza del Campidoglio, Rome

Medici Chapel, which anyway replaced the monument in Michelangelo's interest. The schemes were interchangeable to such an extent that in the final arrangement two sculptures (the Medici *Madonna* and *Leah*) were probably transferred from one project to the other.

Whatever the precise programme of the sculpture—and it is quite possible that Michelangelo had not finally resolved it—the most significant thing about the Medici Chapel is that the expression of a profound and disturbing meaningfulness was achieved not solely by the use of pictorial figurative symbols, but also by the use of architectural elements—windows, pilasters, capitals, and so on. These were traditionally regarded as inanimate functional elements which might be enlivened by applied decoration. Michelangelo's mature architecture was undecorated and the structure itself was modelled and improvised into an expressive vehicle.

The only mention we have by Michelangelo of his theory of architecture is in a letter which compares a building to a human figure not, as was common in the Renaissance, in its ideal Vitruvian proportions, but in its anatomy (see p. 29). The library which Michelangelo built into San Lorenzo is its outstanding demonstration (figures 3, 4, 5). There is no sculpture in this building, but the architecture is both sculptural and expressive. While the main reading room is a relatively calm, horizontal space with a simple pilaster order on the walls, the vestibule, a vertical shaft of space, is overpowering in its inten-

sity. What makes the vestibule so uncomfortable to stand in is more than its mannerist disregard of traditional Classical forms, for which it is historically very important. Cornices and pediments are freely cut open, columns are squashed back functionless into the wall and exterior tabernacle windows of a very weird sort are applied to an interior wall—and cannot be seen through anyway. This ruthless defiance of tradition contributed enormously to the freedom of later sixteenth-century architects. But what confronts one on entering the vestibule is more than this: it is like being inside a living cell. The walls constantly break back and forward, oppressively heavy in form and with a loud black and white colour contrast that makes the Medici Chapel's strange harmony of pale grey, cream and white seem refined and delicate. Overhead there is no serene relieving dome but a crushingly heavy wooden ceiling, flat and richly carved. The forms seem to bear in upon the space from all sides and against these are set the expanding forces of the staircase which floods down from the reading room doorway almost filling the small floor area. So one is caught in a violent conflict of opposed strenghts and faced with a cascading staircase which it is strenuous even to contemplate ascending. Michelangelo's original contribution to architecture was not only to treat architectural form with the same sculptural freedom that he applied to a marble block, but also to make it live and breathe, to give it that same sense of massive inner forces, both spiritual and physical, that pervades his figures in stone and paint. The violent expressiveness is at its most extreme in the library vestibule, but this organic sense is fundamental to the character of his late architecture.

One might say that Michelangelo's late style spanned the last thirty years of his life. Dating from the moment when he left Florence finally for Rome in 1534, this period includes two major fresco commissions in the Vatican (the *Last Judgement* and the Pauline Chapel), two major architectural commissions (the Piazza del Campidoglio and St Peter's) as well as several others, but almost no completed sculpture. On paper this might seem a poor consummation of a lifetime's work for an artist who claimed repeatedly to be neither an architect nor a painter. It is a measure of his greatness that these works rank among the major achievements in architecture and painting of the mid-sixteenth century and anticipated the art of the seventeenth. The commissions to design the civic and religious centres of

Rome came almost simultaneously (about 1546–47). In both cases he was restricted by existing buildings or foundations and in both cases later additions have modified the character of his design. The second condition applies least to the Piazza del Campidoglio (see note to plate 45), the seat of the government of the city of Rome. Although the façade of the central palace is an extensive departure from Michelangelo's design, the piazza retains its unity. An intimate and serene environment, it is one of the sixteenth century's most remarkable pieces of town planning. Although architectural unorthodoxies (like the giant pilaster spanning both storeys of the side palaces here, or the extraordinary decorative motifs of the Porta Pia) persist, the violence of the Laurenziana vestibule has matured. The swelling rhythms of the pavement pattern which radiate from a gently raised central ellipse are harmoniously contained by the (predetermined) placing of the palaces on three sides of a tapering rectangle (plate 45). Michelangelo conceived the administrative centre of Rome as an island of calm and refinement high above the city. Its character remains unknown to the spectator until he has actually climbed one of the slopes into the square, at which point the piazza suddenly surrounds him in all its completeness. This enforced experience, although more restrained than the library, contains the germ of the Baroque sense of a dramatic, environmental city architecture. The site of the piazza on the Capitoline Hill was chosen for its strong associations with the glory of ancient Rome. The antique-equestrian bronze of Marcus Aurelius, standing as the square's central feature, is the climax of a consciously drawn parallel between the glorious past and the aspirations of the contemporary (Christian) Roman republic.

Michelangelo's lifelong respect for the art and architecture of ancient Rome found its final expression in his design for St Peter's. Like Bramante, who had laid the first foundations in 1506, he envisaged a centrally planned church, itself an ideal Classical form. The dome was to be borne on four colossal piers, free-standing in the sort of vast spatial area that one associates with Roman baths or arenas. Much of this he inherited, but his plan shows (figure 8) that he intended to emphasise the character of a single space unit by merging all subsidiary divisions into the sculptural mass of the wall, leaving only the four piers standing clear. The simplicity of his interior was disguised first by Maderna's addition of the nave and secondly by the extrava-

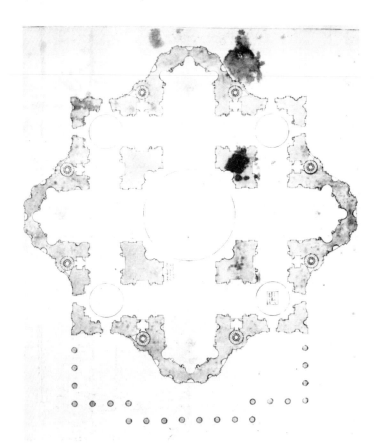

8 Copy of Michelangelo's plan design for St. Peter's, Rome

gance of the seventeenth-century decoration. Severely inhibited by existing construction in the interior of the building, Michelangelo nevertheless succeeded in completely determining its outward appearance. Maderna's façade and Bernini's colonnade have since transformed the main public view of the church, but seen from the Vatican gardens in the west, the exterior exists as Michelangelo intended it. The symmetrical main body of the church, again articulated by a giant pilaster order, ripples in and out in a swelling sculptural change of surface, while the heavy armour-plated dome appears to hover above unsupported. The freedom of formal treatment both in detail and in the handling of masses which characterises Michelangelo's architecture exemplifies the unorthodoxy of his whole approach to the medium.

Even less a professional architect than Brunelleschi or Bramante, he is acknowledged by architectural scholars as one of the handful of really original architects that history has known. He resolved his architectural problems with the sculptor's feeling for organic unity, for the play of mass against void and for the expressive power of formal relationships. His own feeling of failure as a sculptor seems not to have taken into account the architectural achievements which realised what were essentially sculptural concepts. These two architectural commissions were the climax of his public career. The painting and sculpture of his last thirty years was the more personal and more closely reflected the mood of his inner feelings.

Michelangelo's early years of permanent residence in Rome

were spiritually the richest of his life. They were enriched by the love and friendship he shared with Vittoria Colonna. He felt a profound spiritual affinity with her and their association helped him to clarify his attitude towards life and God. Religious thought at the time had been deeply disturbed by the Sack of Rome (1527) and this disturbance was intensified by the Counter-Reformation.

The Sack of Rome (eight days of destruction, plunder, murder and rape during which the Pope was besieged, helpless, in Castel Sant' Angelo) was the final act of subjugation suffered by Italy at the hands first of France under Francis I and now of Spain, with the help of German mercenaries, under Charles V. Italy had not been occupied by foreign powers since the Middle Ages, but more devastating even than this was the fact that since the time of Julius II, Rome itself had stood as a symbol of Italian Renaissance culture and as the stronghold of papal authority over a reform-conscious Catholic Church. Its image in both these respects was shattered. The neurotic, unstable character of much Italian Mannerism and the extreme reactionary orthodoxy of the Italian Counter-Reformation both originate in the Sack of Rome.

Colonna was intimately associated with a strong reforming faction within the papal court which was later heavily criticised by the Council of Trent. Michelangelo's religious faith was of a simple unpretentious nature and Vittoria Colonna's conviction in the purity of the soul as the true path towards enlightenment only served to deepen his humility. The paintings, drawings, carvings and sonnets of his last years are characterised by an increasingly violent repudiation of the flesh and a self-effacing, often hopeless yearning after spiritual awakening.

The theme of awakening which recurs in Michelangelo's work—in the *Slaves* for the Julius Tomb, the Medici Chapel allegories, or collectively in the Sistine Ceiling prophets—is always allied to the Neoplatonic concept of the soul's awakening in the form of its liberation from the flesh. In the presentation drawing known as '*The Dream*' (figure 10), the graceful smooth body of the ideal youth is perfect because of this inner revelation and contrasts with the ill-defined, heavy groups beyond, which represent the sins of the flesh.

When Michelangelo was asked by Pope Paul III to decorate the altar wall of the Sistine Chapel, he chose to paint a *Last Judgement* (plate 38), a subject both unprecedented and unemu-lated for such a position. As a subject it is of course the climax to any theme of the soul's redemption and the damnation of weakness. For Michelangelo there was the added significance of its relationships to the Sistine Ceiling's theme of Salvation and to the Chapel's altar, which is starkly set against the blackest regions of hell. It is one of the most pessimistic Last Judgements in the history of European painting: its true ancestors lie in medieval sculpture. Christ is a furious threatening figure, his arm raised in condemnation, and the supporting saints Peter and John are not pleading intercessors, but stern prosecutors urging Christ to severity. The fall of the damned on the right is a tumultuous, violent descent: their fall is hastened not so much by symbolic devils (although they are here in medieval strength) as by their own faithless despair. Salvation is very hard won. The ascent of the saved souls on the left is not the traditional serene rise of the blessed to the Garden of Paradise, but a hazardous grim struggle for survival. In this lies the real innovation. An artist of the Renaissance like Signorelli had anticipated Michelangelo in the physical violence of his Hell in the frescoes in Orvieto Cathedral (about 1499). But he contrasted this with the optimistic idealisation of his muscular blessed souls, strolling in Paradise, bathed in Salvation. In Michelangelo's *Judgement* there is no such clear distinction: the ascending souls seem liable to fall again should the concentration of their struggle slacken even momentarily. Nowhere is physical beauty glorified with the ideal humanist self-confidence of the Sistine Ceiling's supernatural world: the body is heavy and cumbersome, floundering through a succession of helpless poses which repeatedly state its inadequacy. By contrast with the ceiling decoration's built-in architectural stability, the composition of the *Last Judgement* is fluid and structureless. In painting, Michelangeo's new organic sense of form was un-fettered by any functional demands. Not only does he abandon the hieratic sense of order traditional to this subject, but the integrity of the wall surface is destroyed; there is no co-ordinated viewpoint, no trompe l'oeil, no painted frame even. The heaving swarms of figures swim, float or sink against an infinite space, with a generalised sense of circular movement around the central group.

The *Last Judgement* was unveiled to a very mixed reception in October 1541 and was immediately followed by the papal com-mission to decorate the Pauline Chapel. In despair Michelangelo wrote: 'I shall paint with discontent and my work shall arouse discontent.' His reluctance towards the commission was deepened by his grief at Vittoria Colonna's death in 1547. The *Conversion of Saul* (plate 43) is a violent asymmetrical drama, but the *Crucifixion of St Peter* (plate 44) is far less positive in character. The formal ambiguity of the high viewpoint and contradictions of scale reflect the extraordinary mood of the doubting, whispering, curious or brooding circle of spectators. This strangeness builds up to a peak in the figure of St Peter, who, almost at the moment of his crucifixion, turns and stares questioningly, perhaps accusingly, straight out of the painting towards us. Clearly these, his last paintings, are deeply personal expressions and the images with which he identified himself are even more pessimistic, by virtue of their uncertainty, than the *Last Judgement*.

The growing subordination of individual parts which was apparent in the last stages of the Sistine Ceiling reached a peak in these last frescoes. Whereas the ceiling was made up of individually considered units, the *Last Judgement* (like the plan of St Peter's) is united in a single organisation. Increasingly, Michelangelo grew more concerned with the direct expression of a single theme and less interested in either the perfection of the component parts or the finish of the whole. The most powerful evidence of this is the unfinished state of at least half of his sculpture. The *Slaves* (plate 25) which were made for the Julius Tomb and later withdrawn, obviously unfinished, are widely recognised as amongst his most expressive works. In them the intensity of feeling is unspoilt by the artifice of a high imitative finish. This is not just romanticism. The general subordination of external perfection to inner intensity (which is evident even in the finished statues of *Rachel* and *Leah*) suggests that in the *Slaves* the main artistic problems had for Michelangelo already been solved. In reaching this stage he had accomplished the major act of creation and all that remained was the comparatively mechanical act of dressing it suitably for public appearance. Once he had proved to his public and to himself (in his early works) his supreme technical mastery, he was relatively unconcerned with this aspect of his art. Apparently the *Moses* stood in Michelangelo's studio in a comparable state for many years and was only 'finished' at the last moment. In the last *Pietà* he seems to have found it impossible to realise the depth of his feeling in any conventional physical form.

The unfinished sculptures also have the character of free-standing reliefs. Very often (for example in the St Matthew, the Slaves, the Medici Madonna, the Palestrina Pietà) the back of the block is barely cut into and in this way each sculpture, like a relief, maintains its double identity as stone and as image. Most of his sculpture was conceived from a single or limited viewpoint and made to stand near or against an architectural setting, as a relief is applied to a surface. In the only really freestanding figure, the *Bacchus*, he closely respected the shape of the block and in a sonnet of the 1540s (see page 29) he put into words the now popular concept of his figures already existing within the block only waiting to be uncovered by the chisel. This relief character is so closely echoed both in his painting (the overlapping groups against a spatially ambiguous background in the Pauline Chapel, for example) and in his architecture (the way his vigorous surface modelling appears to grow out of the walls), that the 'unfinished' sculptures seem more in keeping with his oeuvre as a whole than those that are highly finished. They are not only a complete statement spiritually and expressively, they suggest that he was also conscious of a satisfying formal balance in them between the inanimate marble and the half-emerged image which would (like the intensity of expression) be similarly lost in a high finish.

This denial of a complete three-dimensionality in his art becomes the perfect manifestation of the spiritual development of his last years and is revealed most clearly in the fluid, painterly late drawings and the three late *Pietàs*. These were all uncommissioned works, undertaken out of his own desire or compulsion to create them: he apparently intended the Florentine *Pietà* (with its long-attributed self-portrait in the figure of Nicodemus) for his own tomb. Uninhibited by the standards of craftsmanship of his public successes, Michelangelo finally succeeded in expressing that inner force which had seemed to struggle against physical weight and mass in the *St Matthew* and the *Slaves*. In the drawings, the masses dematerialise as if consumed from within. It was only in a total repudiation of all the artistic values the Renaissance had stood for—not least its rationality and formal strength—that Michelangelo groped his way towards an art capable of expressing intense religious humility.

All three *Pietàs* were left unfinished. One he partially destroyed; and another, the Rondanini (plate 51), he reworked to a point of total transformation, not bothering to eliminate the ambiguous fragments of his first conception which still remain. The group in Florence Cathedral (plate 49) is the earliest of the three and the most dynamic in its jagged composition: this physical character must have been more emphatic before he destroyed the left leg of Christ which was thrust out over the Virgin's thigh. The monumental Palestrina *Pietà* (plate 50), its lumbering mass swaying on Christ's lifeless legs, is already irrationally unstable and coalescent. The spiritual power of the image seems to transcend its dragging weight and rises up through Christ's body to reach a climax in the moving closeness of the heads.

In the Rondanini *Pietà* the group is reduced to two figures and almost to one as mother and son merge together into an ascending, weightless arc. In the economy of figures it recalls the St Peter's *Pietà* of sixty years earlier. But everything he valued in that early masterpiece—the superlative craftsmanship, the impeccably decorous restraint, the sense of monumental plasticity, the confident humanist faith in physical perfection— is sacrified in the Rondanini. John Pope-Hennessy has described it as 'a symbolic act of suicide': for Michelangelo it must have been not only a confession of his religious faith, but also a last confession of what he believed to be his failure as a sculptor. Not since the *David* of 1504 had a sculpture commission been completed in a form that even approached his aspirations. Paradoxically, outward success of his public career—he was retained by successive popes through most of his life—and of his completed achievements as architect and painter was responsible for the frustration and sense of failure that it conceals. The constant and evergrowing demands of patrons (Francis I of France and Henry VIII of England were among the disappointed) were a hindrance, and even when they became pleading in proportion to the growing recognition of his genius he was not temperamentally suited to enjoy or exploit this position of strength.

Far from resting on his laurels, he still needed to fulfil himself in his own eyes and only desired the time and solitude to do so. This tormenting situation was heightened at the end by the self-reproaching confusion of his religious faith, thinking his life to have been wasted and rejecting his Neoplatonic beliefs as misguided (although in fact they closely anticipated the pure spirituality of his Christian faith). The anguish of his uncertainty is belied by the generous, considerate nature revealed in most of

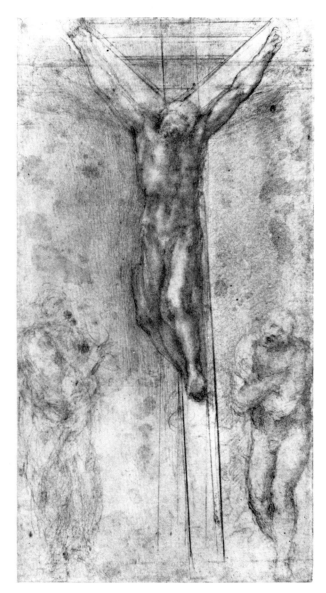

9 Michelangelo: Christ on the Cross with the Virgin and St. John

his letters and by the socially sought-after man described by his devoted friends. It is only in his art—particularly his late sonnets and carvings—that this intensity of feeling (the *terribilità* for which he was renowned) is released. The Rondanini *Pietà*, which he was still carving within days of his death, is the most ecstatic religious image produced in a century that included Grünewald and El Greco.

The whole development of Michelangelo's art closely reflects the evolution of his character and convictions: this accounts for its extraordinary homogeneity. But, partly because of the styleless immediacy of the unfinished works, it nevertheless has a timeless and universal quality. To its changing character the history of art owes not only the supreme consummation of the Italian Renaissance, but also an extension of the expressive language of painting, sculpture and architecture that is not remotely anticipated by the Renaissance and only seldom as fully exploited since.

Biographical list of works

This list includes works not illustrated in this book and the most important lost works as well as brief biographical notes. In the case of drawings, only those illustrated and others of particular importance are listed.

Florence: 1475 to October 1494

1475	(March 6th) Michelangelo (Michel Agniolo Buonarroti) born at Caprese, near Florence.
1488	Apprenticeship to Ghirlandaio, lasting only a few months.
c. 1488	Copy after Schongauer's engraving of *The Temptation of St Anthony*. (Tempera on panel. Lost?) See page 25
c. 1488–90	Drawings: Copies after Giotto, Masaccio and the antique. **Figure 2**
1488/89	Enters the Medici sculpture school under Bertoldo.
1490–92	Member of the Medici household.
c. 1491	*Madonna of the Stairs*. (Marble relief. Casa Buonarroti, Florence.) **Plate 1**
c. 1492	*Battle of the Centaurs*. (Marble relief. Casa Buonarroti, Florence.)
c. 1492	*Crucifixion*. (Wood. Lost?) See page 25
c. 1492–94	*Hercules*. (Marble. Lost.)

Venice and Bologna: October 1494 to Autumn 1495

1494–95	Three marble figures (*St Petronius, St Proculus* and an angel. San Domenico, Bologna).

Florence: Autumn 1495 to June 1496

1494/96	*St John*. (Marble. Lost?) See page 25
1495/96	*Cupid*. (Marble. Lost.)

Rome: June 1496 to May 1501

c. 1496	*Apollo*. (Marble. Lost.)
c. 1497	*Bacchus*. (Marble. Bargello, Florence.) **Plate 2**
1498	Visit to the quarries at Carrara.
1498–99	*Pietà*. (Marble. St Peter's Rome.) **Plate 3**

Florence: May 1501 to March 1505

1501	Commission for fifteen marble statues, Piccolomini Altar, Siena Cathedral. (Only five were designed and possibly partly executed by Michelangelo.)
1501–4	*David*. (Marble. Accademia, Florence.) **Plates 4, 5, 19**
1502–8	*David*. (Bronze. Lost.)
c. 1503–4	*Holy Family—Doni Tondo*. (Tempera on panel. Uffizi, Florence.) **Plate 6**
c. 1504–5	*Madonna and Child*. (Marble. Notre-Dame, Bruges.)
c. 1504–5	*Madonna and Child—Pitti Tondo*. (Marble relief. Bargello, Florence.)
c. 1505–6	*Madonna and Child—Taddei Tondo*. (Marble relief. Royal Academy, London.) **Plate 7**
c. 1505–6	*Battle of Cascina*. (Cartoon. Lost.) **Figure 1**

Rome: March 1505 to April 1506

1505	Commission and first designs for the *Tomb of Julius II*.
1505	(May to November) Selection of marble for the tomb at Carrara.

Florence: April to November 1506

c. 1506	*St Matthew*. (Marble. Accademia, Florence.) **Plate 8**

Bologna: November 1506 to February 1508

1506–8	
1508	*Statue of Julius II*. (Bronze. Destroyed 1511.) (February) Michelangelo returned to Florence.

Rome: Spring 1508 to July 1516

1508–12	Vault frescoes, Sistine Chapel, Rome. **Plates 9, 10, 11-21**
1513	Death of Julius II: Second Contract for the Tomb.
c. 1513–16	*Moses* for Julius II Tomb. (Marble.) **Plate 23**
	Dying Slave, Rebellious Slave for Julius II Tomb. (Marble. Louvre, Paris.) **Plate 24**
1514	Exterior, Leo X Chapel, Castel Sant' Angelo, Rome.

1516	Third contract for the Julius II Tomb.

Florence: July 1516 to September 1534

c. 1516–20	Designs for the façade of San Lorenzo, Florence. Abandoned 1520.
c. 1516–34	*Victory* for Julius II Tomb. (Marble. Palazzo Vecchio, Florence..)
c. 1517	Ground-floor windows designed for Palazzo Medici, Florence.
c. 1519–20	*Risen Christ.* (Marble. Santa Maria sopra Minerva, Rome.)
1520–34	Medici Chapel, San Lorenzo, Florence. **Figure 6. Plates 27–37**
1524	Library, San Lorenzo, Florence. **Figures 3–5**
c. 1525	*David* (or *Apollo*). (Marble. Bargello, Florence.)
1527	Sack of Rome by the troops of Emperor Charles V.
1528–29	Designs for the fortifications of Florence.
c. 1528–34	Four *Slaves* for Julius II Tomb. (Marble. Accademia, Florence.) **Plates 25, 26**
1529	(July to November) Visit to Ferrara and Venice.
1529–30	*Leda and the Swan.* (Tempera on panel. Lost.)
c. 1530–34	Series of *Resurrection* drawings.
1531–32	*Reliquary Tribune*, San Lorenzo, Florence.
1532–34	Several extended visits to Rome.
1532	Fourth contract for the Julius II Tomb.
1532	Began friendship with Tommaso de' Cavalieri.
c. 1532–33	Presentation drawings for Cavalieri.

Rome: September 1534 to 1564

c. 1536–38	Met Vittoria Colonna.
1536–41	*Last Judgement.* (Fresco. Sistine Chapel, Rome.) **Plates 38–42**
c. 1538–40	Presentation drawings for Julius II Tomb. **Figure 10**
1542	Fifth contract for the Julius II Tomb.
c. 1542–45	*Rachel* and *Leah* (?) for Julius II Tomb. (Marble.) **Plate 22**
1542–50	*Conversion of Saul, Crucifixion of St Peter.* (Frescoes. Pauline Chapel, Rome.) **Plates 43** and **44**
c. 1545	Termination of the *Julius II Tomb* project. (San Pietro in Vincoli, Rome.) **Plate 22**

c. 1546	*Brutus.* (Marble. Bargello, Florence.)
c. 1546–64	Piazza del Campidoglio, Rome. **Figure 7 Plates 45, 46**
1546–64	Completion of Palazzo Farnese, Rome.
1547–64	St Peter's, Rome. **Figure 8. Plate 48**
1547	Death of Vittoria Colonna.
c. 1547–55	*Pietà.* (Marble, Florence Cathedral.) **Plate 49**
1550	First edition of Vasari's *The Lives* published.
1553	Condivi's *Life of Michelangelo* published.
c. 1555–56	Series of *Crucifixion* drawings. **Figure 9**
c. 1552–64	Rondanini *Pietà.* (Marble. Castello Sforzesco, Milan.) **Plates 51, 52**
c. 1555	*Deposition*, (Red chalk. Ashmolean Museum, Oxford.) **Plate 53**
c. 1556	Palestrina *Pietà.* (Marble. Accademia, Florence.) **Plate 50**
1558–59	The nudes of the *Last Judgement* 'made decent' at the order of Pope Paul IV.
1559	Designs for San Giovanni dei' Fiorentini, Rome.
c. 1560	Designs for the Capella Sforza, Santa Maria Maggiore, Rome.
1561–64	Porta Pia, Rome. **Plate 47**
1561–64	Santa Maria degli Angeli, Rome. (Designs for the conversion of the Roman Baths of Diocletian.)
1564	(February 18th) Death of Michelangelo.

Several attempts have been made during this century to identify existing works with those by Michelangelo that were mentioned in the early literary sources (Vasari, Condivi and others) but have since disappeared. Two of the most recent attributions are particularly worth mentioning. An impressive seated *St John* (marble, 40½ in. high; 103 cm.) now in the collection of Piero Tozzi, New York, has been identified by some as the *St John* of 1495–96 and a *Crucifixion* (painted wood, 53 in. high; 134.5 cm.) that had hung for a long time in the Friary of Santo Spirito, Florence has been identified as the early crucifix carved by Michelangelo for that church; it has recently been on exhibition in the Casa Buonarroti, Florence.

A panel, purporting to be the early copy of Schongauer's *Temptation of St Anthony*, was auctioned at Sotheby's in December 1960. It was purchased for a private collection for £13,000.

There are a few unconvincing attributions of paintings (mostly in private collections) which have not been included in this list. Some scholars claim to have recognised his youthful hand in Ghirlandaio's frescoes in Santa Maria Novella, Florence (1488). The best of the falsely attributed panel paintings are the two unfinished works in the National Gallery, London: a *Madonna and Child with St John* and an *Entombment*.

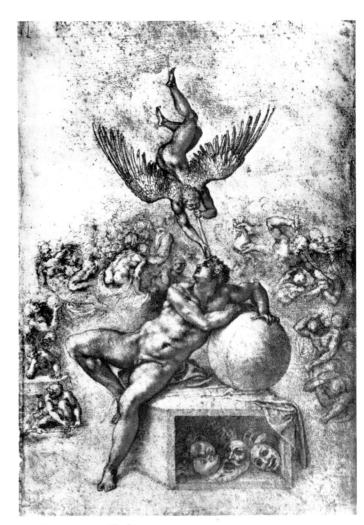

10 Michelangelo: *The Dream*

OTHERS ON MICHELANGELO

While the most noble and industrious spirits were striving, by the light of the famous Giotto and of his followers, to give to the world proof of their ability, the Ruler of Heaven in His clemency sent down to earth a spirit with universal ability in every art, who might be able, working by himself alone, to show what manner of thing is the perfection of the art of design in executing the lines, contours, shadows and high lights, so as to give relief to works of painting, and what it is to work with correct judgement in sculpture, and how in architecture it is possible to render habitations secure and commodious, healthy and cheerful, well proportioned, and rich with varied ornaments. He was pleased, in addition, to endow him with the true moral philosophy and with the ornament of sweet poesy, to the end that the world might choose him and admire him as its highest exemplar in the life, works, saintliness of character, and every action of human creatures, and that he might be acclaimed by us as being rather divine than human . . .

Now to be brief, I must record that the master's constitution was very sound, for he was lean and well knit together with nerves, and although as a boy he was delicate, and as a man he had two serious illnesses, he could always endure any fatigue and had no infirmity, save that in his old age he suffered from dysuria and from gravel, which in the end developed into the stone; wherefore for many years he was syringed by the hand of Maestro Realdo Colombo, his very dear friend, who treated him with great diligence. He was of middle stature, broad in the shoulders, but well proportioned in all the rest of his body. In his latter years he wore buskins of dogskin on the legs, next to the skin, constantly for whole months together, so that afterwards, when he sought to take them off, on drawing them off the skin often came away with them. Over the stockings he wore boots of cordwain fastened on the inside, as a protection against damp. His face was round, the brow square and spacious, with seven straight lines, and the temples projected considerably beyond the face, or rather on the large side; the nose was somewhat flattened; having been broken, as was said, by Torrigiano; the eyes rather on the small side, of the colour of horn, spotted with bluish and yellow gleams; the eyebrows with few hairs, the lips thin, with the lower lip rather thicker and projecting a little, the chin well shaped and in proportion with the rest, the hair black, but mingled with white hairs, like the beard, which was not

very long, forked, and not very thick.
Vasari, *Life of Michelangelo.* 1568.

I already knew that in everything you follow the doctrine of the Lord: *deposuit potentes, exaltavit humiles*; and in that also you are excellent, for you acknowledge yourself at last as discreetly generous and not as an ignorant prodigal. And therefore in Rome those who know you esteem you even more than your works; and those who do not know you esteem only the least of you, which are the works of your hands. And certainly I do not give any less praise to your knowledge of how to retire within yourself and fly from our useless conversations, and to your wisdom in not painting for all the princes who ask you to do so, but confining yourself to the painting of a single work during all your life as you have done.
Vittoria Colonna to Michelangelo, in the *First Dialogue of Francisco d'Ollanda.* 1538.

I saw Michelangelo at work. He had passed his sixtieth year and although he was not very strong, yet in a quarter of an hour he caused more splinters to fall from a very hard block of marble than three young masons in three or four times as long . . . And he attacked the work with such energy and fire that I thought it would fly into pieces. With one blow he brought down fragments three or four fingers in breadth, and so exactly at the point marked, that if only a little more marble had fallen he would have risked spoiling the whole work.
Blaise de Vigenère. 1550

MICHELANGELO ON HIMSELF

I've grown myself a goitre at this chore,
As water gives the cats in Lombardy
Or in whatever land it be,
And it shoves my stomach under my chin by force.

My beard towards heaven, I feel my nape support
The back of my head, I grow the breast of a harpy
And my brush as it drips continually
Upon my face, makes it a gorgeous floor.

My loins have got squeezed into my paunch,
The counterweight, a crupper, is my rump;
Pointless, without my eyes, each step I go.

My skin behind, by folding, is all bunched,
While it is getting pulled out long in front,
And I am stretched out like a Syrian bow.

So the judgements will grow
False and bizarre, that form within my brain:
A twisted gun cannot be rightly aimed.

So you must now defend,
John, both my dead painting and my honour.
I being in no good place, and not a painter.

I' o gia facto un gozo in questo stento,
  Come fa l'aqua a gacti in Lonbardia
  Over d'altro paese che si sia,
  Ch'a frza 'l ventre apicha octo 'l mento.

La barba al cielo e la memoria sento
  In sullo scrignio e 'l ecto so d'arpia,
  E 'l pennel sopra 'l viso tuctavia
  Mel fa gocciando un richo avimento.

E lombi entrati mi son nella peccia,
  E fo del cul per chontrapeso groppa,
  E passi senza gli ochi muovo invano.

Dinanzi mi s' allunga la chorteccia
  E per piegarsi adietro si ragroppa,
  E tendomi com' archo soriano.

Pero fallace e strano
Surgie il iuditio, che la ente porta,
Che mal si tra' per cerboctana torta.

La mia pictura morta
Difendi orma', Giovanni, e 'l mio onore,
Non sendo in loco bon ne io pictore.

Sonnet written for Giovanni da Pistoia. 1511. (This amusing self-portrait describes his physical condition while painting the Sistine Ceiling.)

There are many persons who maintain a thousand lies, and one is that eminent painters are eccentric and that their conversation is intolerable and harsh, they are only human all the while, and thus fools and unreasonable persons consider them fantastic and fanciful, allowing them with much difficulty the conditions necessary to a painter . . . foolish, idle persons are unreasonable in expecting so many compliments from a busy man . . .

. . . painters are not in any way unsociable through pride, but either because they find few pursuits equal to painting, or in order not to corrupt themselves with the useless conversation of idle people, and debase the intellect from the lofty imaginations in which they are always absorbed. And I affirm . . . that even His Holiness annoys and wearies me when at times he talks to me and asks me somewhat roughly why I do not come to see him, for I believe that I serve him better in not going when he asks me, little needing me, when I wish to work for him and others.

Michelangelo to Vittoria Colonna, in the *First Dialogue of Francisco d'Ollanda*. 1538.

MICHELANGELO ON ART

In my opinion painting should be considered excellent in proportion as it approaches the effect of relief, while relief should be considered bad in proportion as it approaches the effect of painting. I used to consider that sculpture was the lantern of painting and that between the two things there was the same difference as that between the sun and the moon. But now that I have read your book, in which, speaking as a philosopher, you say that things which have the same end are themselves the same, I have changed my opinion. And I now consider that painting and sculpture are one and the same thing, unless greater nobility be imparted by necessity for a keener judgement, greater difficulties of execution, stricter limitations and harder work. And if this be the case no painter ought to think less of sculpture than of painting and no sculptor less of painting than of sculpture. By sculpture I mean the sort that is executed by cutting away from the block: the sort that is executed by building up resembles painting . . .

As to that man* who wrote saying that painting was more noble than sculpture, as though he knew as much about it as he did of the other subjects on which he has written, why, my serving maid would have written better! An infinite number of things remain to be said which might be urged in favour of these arts, but, as I have already said, they would take up too much

*This is probably a reference to Leonardo who described sculpture as 'mechanical exercise'.

time and I have very little to spare seeing that I am old and almost fitted to be numbered among the dead.
Letter to Benedetto Varchi. 1547.

They paint in Flanders only to deceive the external eye, things that gladden you and of which you cannot speak ill, and saints and prophets. Their painting is of stuffs, bricks and mortar, the grass of the fields, the shadows of the trees, and bridges and rivers, which they call landscapes, and little figures here and there; and all this, although it may appear good to some eyes, is in truth done without reasonableness or art, without symmetry or proportion, without care in selecting or rejecting, and finally without any substance or verve . . . Only works done in Italy can be called true painting, and therefore we call good painting Italian, for if it were done so well in another country, we should give it the name of that country or province. As for the good painting of this country, there is nothing more noble and devout . . . because good painting is nothing else but a copy of the perfections of God and a reminder of His painting. Finally, good painting is a music and a melody which intellect only can appreciate, and with great difficulty. This painting is so rare that few are capable of doing it or attaining to it.
Michelangelo to Vittoria Colonna, in the *First Dialogue of Francisco d'Ollanda*. 1538.

. . . the painter . . . not only will be instructed in liberal arts and other sciences such as architecture and sculpture which are his province, but also in all other manual crafts which are practised throughout the world; should he wish, he will do them with more art than the actual masters of them. However that may be, I sometimes set myself thinking and imagining that I find amongst men but one single art or science, and that is drawing or painting, all others being members proceeding therefrom.
Michelangelo to Lactanio Tolomei, in the *Second Dialogue of Francisco d'Ollanda*. 1538.

Design, which by another name is drawing, and consists of it, is the fount and body of painting, sculpture and architecture and of every other kind of art, and the root of all sciences. Let whoever may have attained to so much as to have the power of drawing know that he holds a great treasure.

Michelangelo to Lactanio Tolomei, in the *Third Dialogue of Francisco d'Ollanda*. 1538.

Just as cutting away, O lady, makes
In stone craggy and rough
A figure come to life,
And grow the larger as the stone grows small,
In the same way good works
For the still trembling soul
Are hidden by the surplus of the flesh,
Whose cover is rough and coarse.
This from my outer shell
You only can release;
In me there is for me no will nor force.

Si come per levar, Donna, si pone
In pietra alpestra e dura
Una viva figura,
Che là piu crescie, u' piu la pietra scema,
Tal alcun' opre buone
Per l'alma, che pur trema,
Cela il superchio della propria carne
Col inculta sua cruda e dura scorza.
Tu pur dalle mie streme
Parti puo' sol levarne,
Ch' in me non è di me voler ne forza.

Sonnet. (Probably composed for Vittoria Colonna, and therefore about 1538–47.)

When a plan has diverse parts all those that are of the same character and dimension must be decorated in the same way and in the same manner; and their counterparts likewise. But when a plan changes its form entirely it is not only permissible, but necessary to vary the ornament also and [that of] their counterparts likewise. The central features are always as independent as one chooses—just as the nose being in the middle of the face, is related neither to one eye nor to the other, though one hand is certainly related to the other and one eye to the other, owing to their being at the sides and having counterparts.

It is therefore indisputable that the limbs of architecture are derived from the limbs of man. No one who has not been or is not a good master of the human figure, particularly of anatomy, can comprehend this.

Letter to an unknown recipient. About 1550. (It was probably written with reference to his plans for St Peter's.)

Poets and painters have power to dare, I mean to dare to do whatever they may approve of; and this good insight and this power they have always had, for whenever a great painter (which very seldom happens) does a work which appears to be false and lying, that falsity is very true, and if he were to put more truth into it it would be a lie, as he will never do a thing which cannot be in itself . . .

But should he, in order better to retain the decorum of place and time, alter some of the limbs (as in a grotesque work, which without that would indeed be without grace and therefore false) or a part of one thing into another species . . . this, although it may appear false can only be called well imagined. The reason is, it is better decoration when, in painting, some monstrosity is introduced for variety and a relaxation of the senses and to attract the attention of mortal eyes, which at times desire to see that which they have never yet seen . . .

And I wish to tell you, Francisco d'Ollanda, of an exceedingly great beauty in this science of ours . . . namely, that what one has most to work and struggle for in painting is to do the work with a great amount of labour and sweat in such a way that it may afterwards appear, however much it was laboured upon, to have been done almost quickly and almost without any labour, and very easily, although it was not.
Michelangelo, in the *Third Dialogue of Francisco d'Ollanda.* 1538.

Man's supreme felicity and ultimate beatitude consist in under-standing, in loving and in serving God perfectly . . . in his medi-tation on death, Michelangelo attained his ultimate perfection, his ultimate felicity and his ultimate beatitude . . .

Who ever was more religious? Who ever lived a more godly life? Who ever died a more Christian death than Buonarroti?
Benedetto Varchi. *Orazione.* 1564.

Notes on the illustrations

In the case of architectural projects which were already started before Michelangelo's participation, the date given at the head of the entry refers only to the period of his work on them. The following books are referred to in the notes and are recommended for more detailed study—Charles de Tolnay, *Michelangelo*. Volumes I–V. Princeton University. 1943–1960. Johannes Wilde, *Italian Drawings in the British Museum, Michelangelo and his Studio*. London 1953. James S. Ackerman, *The Architecture of Michelangelo*. London. 1961. John Pope-Hennessy, *Italian High Renaissance and Baroque Sculpture*. London. 1963.

BLACK AND WHITE ILLUSTRATIONS

Figure 1 Aristotile da Sangallo: Copy of Michelangelo's *Battle of Cascina* cartoon. 1542. Tempera on panel (Grisaille). 30 × 51 in. (76 × 129 cm.). Collection of the Earl of Leicester, Holkham Hall.

The most complete extant copy of Michelangelo's cartoon, this is widely believed to represent the whole of the original composition. Its authenticity is supported by several independent copies of smaller fragments of the original (although two of these show further very similar figures in the background) illustrated in Tolnay Vol. I, pl. 233–5. Around 1504 (the contract is lost) Piero Soderini, Gonfaloniere of Florence, commissioned Michelangelo to decorate a section of wall in the Gran' Sala del Consiglio of the Palazzo Vecchio. Leonardo's painting *The Battle of Anghiari*, to which this was to be a pendant, had been commissioned in 1503, was started 1505 and abandoned in May 1506. Michelangelo received payments in connection with the cartoon in 1504 and 1505 and he later recalled (in a letter of 1524) that he had finished it before he left for Rome in March 1505. Some scholars ignore this in believing that the cartoon was executed on his return (that is to say, between April and November 1506). Stylistically it could belong to either period and may belong to both. It is doubtful that he ever started work on the fresco. The walls that he and Leonardo were to decorate are now covered with Vasari's battle frescoes (1567–71). Michelangelo's cartoon was placed in the Council Hall (1508–12), then the Sala del Papa (1512–15) and finally in the Medici Palace (1515–16). It became a model for all young Florentine artists, called the 'school of the world' by Cellini, who considered that Michelangelo never surpassed it. Around 1516 it was cut into pieces, presumably by the copyists, and was quickly dispersed.

Fragments were recorded at Mantua, where Rubens saw them (1604–6), and at Turin as late as 1635, but none exists today. Sangallo made this copy in 1542 from a complete drawing he had made from the original (at Vasari's suggestion, so Vasari tells us). The battle of Cascina was fought between Pisa and Florence in 1364.

Figure 2 *Three Standing Figures*. Pen drawing. $11\frac{1}{2} \times 7\frac{7}{8}$ in. (29 × 20 cm.). Albertina, Vienna. Cat. III 129 recto.

This is probably a copy after Masaccio's lost fresco in the cloister of Santa Maria del Carmine, Florence (depicting the consecration of that church), and was executed about 1488–90. There are other copies, identical in technique, after the antique, after Giotto's Santa Croce frescoes and after Masaccio's Brancacci Chapel frescoes.

Figures 3, 4 and **5** *Biblioteca Laurenziana, San Lorenzo, Florence*. 1524–34. Elevation of the side wall of the Vestibule; plan and section of the Reading Room and Vestibule; view of the Vestibule staircase.

Michelangelo was commissioned to design and build the library around 1524, and worked on it intermittently until he left Florence in 1534. Built above an existing cloister and extending the church's south transept, the reading room was built by 1525 and the vestibule—up to the main cornice—by 1526. Michelangelo originally intended the vestibule to be the same height as the reading room, with a shallow vault. This plan had to be changed in 1525 and he proposed a flat wooden ceiling with a circular skylight. There was a second alteration about 1526 to satisfy the Pope (who complained that 'one would have to commission two monks to do nothing but wipe off the dust'): the third storey was added to provide light and thus exaggerated the vestibule's odd proportions. It is characteristic of Michelangelo's attitude to architecture that he did not attempt to disguise this oddness but fully exploited it.

Ackerman (text vol., pp. 39–41) points out that the mannerist 'unfunctional' columns are in fact main structural members supporting the hidden piers of the third storey which in turn carry the main roof beams.

Michelangelo left detailed designs for the library's ornament when he left Florence but these were not exclusively followed. In 1558 he supplied a clay model for Ammanati to use in constructing the staircase (which he intended to be wooden). His designs for a triangular rare books study at the far end of the reading room (approved in 1525) were discarded in favour of the present circular room before 1571, when the library was completed and opened.

(Diagrams from B. M. Appollonj, *I monumenti italiani*, fascicolo 2, Rome, 1934.)

Figure 6 *Isometric projection of the Medici Chapel, Florence.* (See note to plates 27–37.) From B. M. Apollonj, *I monumenti italiani*, fascicolo 2, Rome, 1934.

Figure 7 Ground plan of the Piazza del Campidoglio, Rome. (See notes to plates 44 and 45.)

Figure 8 Copy of Michelangelo's plan design for St Peter's, Rome, from the workshop of Antonio Labacco. Ink, chalk and brown wash. 15 × 18 in. (38.2 × 45.8 cm.) Royal Library, Windsor. (See note to plate 48.)

Figure 9 *Christ on the Cross with the Virgin and St John.* Black chalk. $15\frac{3}{4} \times 8\frac{5}{8}$ in. (40 × 22 cm.) Royal Library, Windsor. (Inventory No. 12761.) About 1550–56.
Michelangelo made a large number of drawings of Crucifixion, *Pietà* and Deposition subjects in the 1550s. While they reflect the remorseful guilt of his late religious thoughts they also recall the melancholy which pervades his earliest religious works (see note to plate 1). Some art historians (Tolnay and others) consider many of them as studies for sculpture but, as Pope-Hennessy observes, they have an anti-plastic painterly character that seems fundamentally unrealisable in stone. The drawings allowed him the empirical freedom to concentrate emphasis on certain parts of the image (such as the torso here) and to lose the rest in suggestive half-statements. They are comparable to Leonardo's unfinished paintings in this respect. Leonardo and Michelangelo were the first artists seriously to question, however instinctively, the modern problem of 'finish'.

These drawings are obviously related to the late *Pietàs*: the many alterations, which make the forms appear to change as you look at them, show the same inability to arrive at a—to him —satisfactory single image and the same impulsive improvisatory way of working.

Figure 10 *The Dream* or *The Dream of Human Life*. Black chalk. $15\frac{5}{8} \times 11$ in. (40 × 28 cm.) Collection of Count Antoine Seilern, London.

COLOUR PLATES

Plate 1 *Madonna of the Stairs*. Marble relief. $22 \times 15\frac{3}{4}$ in. (55 × 40 cm.). Casa Buonarroti, Florence. About 1491.
The earliest surviving sculpture by Michelangelo. The relief is remarkable for its shallow carving (the maximum depth is less than one inch) which recalls Donatello's subtle exploitation of the very low relief form (*rilievo schiacciato*). There is also an echo of Donatello in the way the playful, fat children intensify by contrast the solemnity of the Virgin. Her brooding seriousness is clearly prophetic of the tragedy of Christ's Passion: this is amplified by Christ's limply hanging right arm and by the largest background child who clings strenuously to the balustrade as if carrying the cross. The St Peter's *Pietà* reverses this analogy: here the infancy is shadowed by the Passion and there the Passion is relieved by a memory of childhood.

The relief was in the Medici collection from about 1567 to 1617, but has since then been in the Buonarroti family's possession.

Plate 2 *Bacchus*. Marble. Height $72\frac{1}{2}$ in (184 cm.) (including base). Bargello, Florence. About 1497.
Bacchus was probably commissioned by Cardinal Riario (who refused to accept it) and then purchased by Jacopo Galli. It stood amongst a collection of antiques in the garden of Galli's Roman house for many years (it was drawn there by Heemskerk (1532–35), when the right hand was missing: this was restored by 1553, probably by Michelangelo.

The statue has been in the Bargello since 1873.

Plate 3 *Pietà*. Marble. Height 69 in. (175 cm.). St Peter's, Rome. 1498–99.
Commissioned in 1498 by Jean de Villiers de le Groslaye, a French cardinal in Rome (who may have suggested the un-Italian iconography), it is Michelangelo's first religious commission and his only signed work—a fact which perhaps reflects Michelangelo's own feeling of achievement.

Although it has been moved from chapel to chapel over the centuries, the group has always stood in St Peter's.

Plates 4, 5 and **19** *David*. Marble. Height 16 ft. 10½ in. (410 cm.) (incl. base). Accademia, Florence. 1501–4.
Commissioned to stand on a buttress of Florence Cathedral, but on completion it was considered too good and a survey of respected opinions (including those of Leonardo, Botticelli and Perugino) was taken before the site, in front of the Palazzo Vecchio (where a full-size copy still stands), was chosen—against the majority vote which was for a site in the Loggia dei Lanzi. Michelangelo had already completed an over-lifesize Hercules, now lost, and the confident scale of these works must reflect the intensive anatomical study on which he was engaged from 1492. (Vasari says that the early wooden crucifix was made for Santo Spirito in payment for the use of a room there (for the dissection of corpses). The block of marble from which *David* was carved was first blocked out by Agostino di Duccio in 1463 and then left. Antonio Rosselino failed to fulfil his commission to complete the giant in 1476. The technical accomplishment of his Roman work must have encouraged the Operai (the administrative body of the Cathedral) to commission Michelangelo to overcome the problem in September 1501. Its completion by April 1504, using no additional stone, seemed little short of miraculous.

The left arm was broken into three pieces during a political disturbance of 1527 (a chair was thrown out of a Palazzo Vecchio window). Vasari and Salviati collected the pieces which were later restored. The figure was moved from its original site to the Accademia in 1873.

Plate 6 *The Holy Family* (The Doni Tondo). Tempera on panel. Diameter 47¼ in. (120 cm.). Uffizi, Florence. About 1503–4.
Commissioned by Agnolo Doni, a well-known Florentine merchant and patron of the arts, possibly in connection with his wedding to Maddalena Strozzi in the winter of 1503–4. On completion he was not satisfied with the painting: a drawn-out dispute about payment followed.

This is Michelangelo's first known painting and the only extant panel painting by him. The male nudes in the background—patently superfluous to the subject—foreshadow the *ignudi* of the Sistine Ceiling.

The painting was already in the Uffizi early in the seventeenth century.

Plate 7 *Madonna and Child with St John* (The Taddei Tondo). Marble relief. Diameter 46¼ in. (117.5 cm.). Royal Academy, London. About 1505–6.
Commissioned by Taddeo Taddei; the contract is lost.

Like all of Michelangelo's Madonnas, the Virgin is solemn and lost in contemplation. Any narrative contexts that he introduces never extend beyond a superficial level and the gravity of these images always indicates a deep consideration of the subject in all its aspects and particularly in its graver implications. (Christ's impulsive fear of the goldfinch held by St John has been interpreted as another anticipation of the Passion.)

Like the smaller relief (the *Pitti Tondo*) in the Bargello, it is unfinished. It was purchased in Rome by Sir George Beaumont in 1823 and later presented by him to the Royal Academy.

Plate 8 *St Matthew*. Marble. Height of block 8 ft. 11 in. (271 m.). Accademia, Florence. About 1506.
Michelangelo was commissioned in April 1503 to make twelve over-lifesize (4¼ *braccia*) figures of the Apostles for the Cathedral in Florence, to be completed within twelve years. Five blocks of marble were quarried at Carrara in 1504, but Michelangelo had already left for Rome before they arrived in Florence. He worked on it on his return in 1506 but it remained unfinished.

As discussed in the introduction, the *St Matthew* almost certainly reflects his reaction to the discovery of the antique sculpture of Laocoön and his two sons in Rome in January 1506. Michelangelo apparently arrived at the scene within hours of its excavation.

The *St Matthew* was in the Opera del Duomo until 1834, when it was moved to the Accademia.

The commission for the twelve Apostles was later divided between six other artists (Jacopo and Andrea Sansovino, Bandinelli, Bandini, Ferrucci and Benedetto da Rovezzano).

Plates 9–18, 20 and **21** *The Sistine Chapel Ceiling*. Vatican, Rome. Fresco. 1508–12.

Julius II first considered this project in 1506 and in May 1508 contracted Michelangelo to replace the existing decoration (blue with gold stars) with twelve Apostles. Michelangelo considered that his own first drawings for this project 'appeared rather mean' and it was probably at his suggestion that the Pope issued a second contract in June 1508. Michelangelo wrote of this later 'then he (Julius) gave me a new commission to make what I wanted, whatever would please me' (letter of 1523). The traditional story of the Pope being persuaded (by Bramante and/or others) to force Michelangelo into a commission which he would not or could not complete is probably largely myth. On the face of it, it seems more likely that Bramante would try to dissuade the Pope from the project altogether. The stories of troublesome assistants are also over-coloured: the few that he employed were his only close social contacts during this period. Michelangelo accepted all of his big fresco commissions with reluctance, but having agreed to undertake them he devoted all of his energies to them and in the event these were the only major projects he saw through to completion.

The scaffolding for the first half of the ceiling was erected in July 1508 and this section (from the entrance wall up to and including the *Creation of Eve*) was finished in 1510 and unveiled in August 1511. The second scaffolding was erected in 1511 and the whole ceiling unveiled in October 1512. Michelangelo rejected Bramante's system of suspending scaffolding since this would have left holes in the ceiling.

The significance of the subject matter is outlined in the introduction. The nine history paintings are arranged as follows (reading from the entrance wall):

The Drunkenness of Noah
The Deluge
The Sacrifice of Noah
The Fall of Man
The Creation of Woman
The Creation of Man
God dividing the Waters from the Earth
The Creation of the Sun and Moon and of the Plants
God dividing the Light from the Darkness

The Chapel was originally divided by a screen (*cancellata*) sepa-rating the clergy from the laity. The arrangement of the histories respected this division: the scenes in which the Creator appeared were all above the clergy's half of the chapel. The screen is no longer in its original position.

The sequence of the three Noah episodes is the reverse of their biblical sequence: the Drunkenness is probably used as a climax to emphasise the final degradation of the flesh to which the histories build up. Throughout Michelangelo shuffles the subject matter with an empirical freedom.

The Prophets and Sibyls are arranged thus: Zechariah (over the entrance) and then in the following facing pairs:

Joel and the Delphic Sibyl
The Erythrean Sibyl and Isaiah
Ezekiel and the Cumaean Sibyl
The Persian Sibyl and Daniel
Jeremiah and the Libyan Sibyl
Jonah (above the altar)

There is a very considerable increase of scale in the last five figures: these belong to the second phase of the ceiling.

Short Notes on the Individual Plates:

Plate 9 General view of the Sistine Chapel showing Michelangelo's *Last Judgement* on the altar wall.

Plate 10 *The Sistine Chapel Ceiling.*

Plate 11 *The Deluge.*
This composition, damaged in 1797, offers a clue as to what the *Battle of Cascina* might have looked like. It represents a similar situation, a moment of great psychological tension.

Plate 12 *The Fall of Man.* (Combining the Temptation and the Expulsion.)
The Eve of the Temptation is the only really sensuous female nude in Michelangelo's oeuvre and the erotic relationship of the two figures is unusual. The introduction of these elements emphasises fleshly weakness. The figures of the Expulsion (reminiscent of Masaccio's Brancacci Chapel fresco) are similarly soft and heavy-bodied by comparison with the perfect Adam of the Creation of Man, creating the same effect.

Plate 13 *The Creation of Man* (see also plate 22).

Plate 14 *The Creation of the Sun and Moon and of the Plants.*
Throughout the sequence *towards* the altar, the figure of Adam becomes more refined and idealised, while the figure of God develops from a benevolent Creator to a furious, commanding image.

Plate 15 *The Libyan Sibyl.*

Plate 16 *Studies for the Libyan Sibyl.* Red chalk. $11\frac{3}{8} \times 8\frac{1}{2}$ in. (28.8 × 19 cm.). Metropolitan Museum of Art, New York, Purchase 1924, Joseph Pulitzer Bequest. About 1511.
Almost all of Michelangelo's studies for figures, whether male or female, were made from a nude male model and his female types with few exceptions tend towards a rather stern masculine grace. Tolnay suggests that in fact he worked to achieve 'a superior beauty which synthesises the beauty of both sexes.' (Vol. II, pp. 60–62).

The repeat drawings of head and torso to the left are probably student copies. There is another study (for the right hand) at Oxford.

It is believed that Michelangelo made clay models for some of the ceiling figures and then drew from them. This would correspond well with his current preoccupation with sculptural values.

Plate 17 *Jeremiah.*

Plate 18 *Jonah.*
The brilliance of Michelangelo's illusionistic perspective reaches a peak in the figure of Jonah, whose body leans back away from the spectator at a point where the wall surface is curving out in precisely the opposite direction. There is a marked similarity between the head of Jonah and the head of the Doni *Madonna* (plate 6): possibly the same study was used.

Plate 19 *David.* Marble. (Detail of Head.) (See notes to plates 4–5.)

Plate 20 *Creation of Man.* (Detail of the head of Adam.)
Comparison of these two heads illustrates well the intervening change in Michelangelo's ideals. *David* (1501–4) stands for the High Renaissance concept of formal perfection in Michelangelo's early Classical period: the figure is outwardly engaged, preoccupied with the physical struggle of life. *Adam* (1511–12)

by comparison is physically listless: his engagement is spiritual and his face expresses an inner intensity.

This detail also shows the facility with which Michelangelo executed the second half of the ceiling. The lines of the cartoon are freely incised in the plaster with a knife or tool and are by no means strictly adhered to.

Plate 21 *An Ignudo.* (Seated above and to the right of the Persian Sibyl.)

Plates 22–26 *The Tomb of Julius II.* Marble. San Pietro in Vincoli, Rome. 1505–45.
The chapter in Condivi's *Life of Michelangelo* which deals with this project is called 'The Tragedy of the Tomb': this undoubtedly reflects Michelangelo's own feelings. He wrote later 'I wasted the whole of my youth on this tomb'. The history of the tomb is as follows:

1505. First Contract. (Lost.)
The initial project was to cost 10,000 ducats and to take five years. It comprised a free-standing two-storey mausoleum occupying 800 square feet of floor space, which could be entered by a door: the sarcophagus was to stand inside. Reconstructions of this design suggest that over forty lifesize marble figures and four large bronze reliefs were involved. The lower storeys were to be decorated with 'bound captives' (the *Slaves*) representing the Liberal Arts, female figures (allegories of the Virtues) and Terms. *Moses* was to be one of four large seated figures on the upper register.

In May, Michelangelo went to Carrara to order vast quantities of marble, which caused a financial crisis in the Vatican when delivered. The Pope had now committed himself to build a new St Peter's—which was probably Michelangelo's suggestion originally—and began to retreat from the tomb scheme. Michelangelo wrote to Julius: 'I was this morning chased out of the Palace on the instructions of your Holiness. I wish to intimate that if from henceforth you require me, you must seek me elsewhere than in Rome', and in February 1506 (shortly before Bramante's foundation stone for the new St Peter's was due to be laid) returned to Florence.

There was a reconciliation with Julius in November 1506 at Bologna, where Michelangelo made a colossal bronze statue of the Pope (which was destroyed by the resentful Bolognese shortly after the Pope's departure).

1513 February 21st: Julius II died.

1513 May. Second Contract. (Drawn up by the Pope's heirs, the della Rovere family, who from now on conducted the negotiations with Michelangelo.)
This project was both a reduction and an expansion. The proposed cost went up from 10,000 to 16,500 ducats and it was to be finished by 1520. The tomb became a wall tomb, the lower storey projecting at right angles to form a long platform two or three bays deep, on which the sarcophagus was now to stand surrounded by four seated figures. The upper storey was heightened to form a tall shallow niche against the wall. The figures were to be fewer (thirty-eight) but larger and now included four saints and a Madonna. The drawings in the Kupferstichkabinett, Berlin, probably represent this project.
Works executed for this project (about 1513–16):
Moses. Marble. Height 8 ft. 4 in. (254 cm.). (Plate 23)
Dying Slave. (Louvre, Paris.) Marble. Height 7 ft. 6½ in. (230 cm.). (Plate 24)
Rebellious Slave. (Louvre, Paris.) Marble. Height 7 ft. 1 in. (216 cm.).
Architecture and decoration of the lower storey which was probably the work of assistants. (The scrolls were added later.) (Plate 22)

1516 July. Third Contract.
This contract constitutes a major reduction to the tomb.

Michelangelo later said it was necessary because of the San Lorenzo façade commission (he was given this in 1516 by Pope Leo X, a Medici and an enemy of the della Rovere). But he was far behind his 1513 schedule anyway, refusing to let assistants execute any of the figures, and must have welcomed this respite. The new project reflects his designs for the San Lorenzo façade. It was for a real wall tomb, one bay deep on both storeys, with even fewer figures (twenty or twenty-four) and eight reliefs. (For works executed for this project, see the fourth contract.)

1532 April. Fourth Contract
There were already discussions around 1525–26 to reduce the project yet again. Michelangelo repeatedly suggested that he

repay the money advanced and wash his hands of it. His enthusiasm was now centred on the Medici Chapel and he had clearly lost interest in the Tomb. The fourth project was again drastically reduced to include only eleven sculptures, six by Michelangelo, and to be erected in San Pietro in Vincoli. Foundations were laid there in 1533. Works executed for this project:
Victory. (Palazzo Vecchio, Florence.) Marble. Height 8 ft. 7½ in. (263 cm.).
Youthful Slave. (Accademia, Florence.) Marble. Height 8 ft. 6¾ in. (261 cm.).
Bearded Slave. (Accademia, Florence.) Marble. Height 8 ft. 8¼ in. (266 cm.).
Atlas. (Accademia, Florence.) Marble. Height 9 ft. 1½ in. (278 cm.). (Plate 25)
Awakening Giant (Accademia, Florence.) Marble. Height 9 ft. (274 cm.). (Plate 26)
   (These five sculptures were carved by Michelangelo in Florence at some time between 1516 and 1534. It is difficult to judge whether they were made for the third or fourth projects, except that just as the Louvre *Slaves* seem close in conception to the figures of the Sistine Ceiling, the Accademia *Slaves* seem related to the style of the *Last Judgement* and probably date from the tail-end of the Florentine period. The *Victory* must be earlier. If, as has been suggested, the Medici *Madonna* was made for the Julius Tomb, it must be contemporary with the *Victory*.)

1542 August. Fifth Contract.
The painting of the *Last Judgement* (1535–41) meant that no further work was undertaken on the Tomb and this final contract was a desperate measure by both sides to compromise and finish the project. Michelangelo was to contribute three autograph figures (*Moses, Rachel* and *Leah*) while the other three (the *Virgin*, a *Sibyl* and a *Prophet*) were to be made by an assistant. (They were carved by Raffaello da Montelupo and one of *his* assistants; the Pope's effigy seems to have been a gratuitous addition.)
Works executed for this project:
Rachel: Marble. Height 6 ft. 7½ in. (202 cm.).
Leah. Marble. Height 6 ft. 10 in. (208.5 cm.). It has been suggested that this figure was first intended for one of the Medici Chapel tombs and was started in the 1529s. Its finished style belongs to the 1540s.

Architecture of the upper storey and scrolls of the lower storey.

The change in his architectural style is if anything more pronounced than that of his sculpture.

1545 February. Completion of the project. (Plate 24)
The tomb was completed as it stands in San Pietro in Vincoli. The unusual sculptures were dispersed. The Louvre *Slaves* were given to Roberto Strozzi and then went to France (in the Louvre since 1794). The Accademia *Slaves* were given to Cosimo I and built into a grotto in the Boboli Gardens (rescued in 1908), and the *Victory*, still in Michelangelo's studio at his death, was considered for his tomb but then placed in the Salone dei Cinquecento of the Palazzo Vecchio.

Plates 27–37 *The Medici Chapel, San Lorenzo, Florence*. 1520–34. The Medici church of San Lorenzo was designed to serve as a place of burial for the family. There were five tombs in the church already, two of them in Brunelleschi's Old Sacristy, to which Michelangelo's chapel was a pendant and whose architecture it consciously revises. The structure of the chapel was already eight months underway when Michelangelo took over and he was left little freedom with the basic shape of the symmetrical building (see figure 6). A professional architect was appointed with him, ostensibly to try to prevent his ambition getting out of hand. He was commissioned (probably by Cardinal Giulio de' Medici) in 1520 to design tombs for Lorenzo the Magnificent (d. 1492) and his brother Giuliano, Duke of Newmours (d. 1516) and Lorenzo, Duke of Urbino (d. 1519), the two 'Capitani'. The first project was for a fairly modest, free-standing monument in the middle of the chapel with a wall tomb on each face. But the project grew in Michelangelo's mind and got sufficiently out of hand to remain unfinished.

The final solution was to have single tombs, one on each side wall, for the Capitani, and a double tomb facing the altar for the Magnifici. The double tomb was never started. It was to include a Madonna and Child and the statues of the Medici patron saints, Cosmas and Damian, that now stand on the ledge facing the altar. The marble *Crouching Boy* in Leningrad probably also belongs to this tomb. The tombs of the Capitani were to be completed by reclining figures of River Gods at the feet of the sarcophagi (there is an autograph clay model for one of them in the Accademia, Florence) and by allegories in the niches beside the Capitani. It has been suggested by several scholars that the *Leah* of the Julius Tomb was first intended as an allegory for the Medici Chapel (and conversely that the Medici *Madonna* was originally made for the Julius Tomb).

The dome was painted with decorative motifs by Giovanni da Udine 1532–33, but these were white-washed in 1556 at Vasari's instruction. Michelangelo's superb studies of the Resurrection of about 1530–34 were possibly made for the frescoes intended on the walls around the altar, or for those of the lunettes above the tombs. The chapel architecture was completed in 1523 and that of the tombs about 1524–27. The eight tabernacles over the doors are closely related to the style of the Laurenziana Library and must also date after 1524.

The most intense periods of activity on the sculpture were 1524–27 and 1530–32. In 1533 three other sculptors (Tribolo, Montelupo and Montosorli) were called in by the Pope to hasten the tombs' completion, but only the patron saints are not by Michelangelo's hand. The Capitani were in position when he left Florence in 1534 and the allegories were placed on the sarcophagi in 1545.

Plates 27, 28 *Views of the Chapel.*

Plates 29, 31 *Tomb of Giuliano de' Medici, Duke of Nemours.* Height of figure 5 ft. 8 in. (173 cm.).

Plates 30, 32 *Tomb of Lorenzo de' Medici, Duke of Urbino.* Height of figure 5 ft. 10 in. (173 cm.).

Plates 33, 35 *Night.* Length of block 6 ft. 4¾ in. (195 cm.). *Day.* Length of block 6 ft. 8¾ in. (205 cm.). Allegories from the tomb of Giuliano.

Plates 34, 36 *Evening.* Length of block 6 ft. 4¾ in. (195 cm.). *Dawn.* Length of block 6 ft. 8 in. (203 cm.). Allegories from the tomb of Lorenzo.

Plate 37 *The Medici Madonna.* Height 7 ft. 5¾ in. (226 cm.).

Plates 38–42 *The Last Judgement.* Fresco. 48 × 44 ft. (14·64 × 13.42 m.). Sistine Chapel, Vatican. 1535–41.
The altar wall of the Sistine Chapel was damaged by fire in 1525. The paintings on the wall at this time were Perugino's altarpiece fresco of the Assumption, two history paintings (completing the 15th-century Old Testament cycle of the other walls)

also by Perugino, the standing figures of Saints Cletus, Linus and Peter and Christ (completing the series of popes) and, above, two lunettes from Michelangelo's ceiling scheme. (The arrangement of these paintings can be gathered from that of the side walls—see plate 9.) The extent of the damage to these paintings is unknown, but it was probably restricted to the lower areas since the original commission to Michelangelo was for a comparatively modest fresco of the Resurrection to replace Perugino's altarpiece. He had recently been preparing for a painting of this subject in the Medici Chapel. The original commission apparently included a Fall of the Rebel Angels for the entrance wall, where the existing paintings had also been accidentally damaged. This second project was dropped when Michelangelo introduced his scheme for the *Last Judgement* to cover the whole altar wall. All the earlier paintings and the cornices were destroyed, the two windows bricked in and the wall replastered (1535–36). The fresco was executed single-handed, with an assistant only to mix colours.

The *Hell* section of the painting includes portraits of two of Michelangelo's critics: Biagio da Cesena (the Papal Master of Ceremonies, who criticised the excessive nudity of the painting during its execution) as Minos, and the poet Pietro Aretino (who gave unwanted advice in 1537, and consequently violently vindicative criticism in 1545) as St Bartholomew. The flayed skin which Bartholomew holds, knife still in hand, has long been recognised as a self-portrait. Vittoria Colonna, Cavalieri, Dante and others have also been tentatively identified.

The unveiling of the *Last Judgement* on October 31st, 1541, was greeted with widespread interest, but also with highly divergent reactions. Aretino's calculated criticisms of impropriety were echoed by the Roman Counter-Reformation. The main defences of the fresco (e.g. by Condivi and Vasari) were in terms of its unrivalled knowledge and use of human anatomy. True recognition of its originality is very recent. (See Tolnay Vol. V pp. 122 ff.)

Plate 38 *The Last Judgement.* (See also plate 9.)

Plate 40 *Detail of the Damned, including Despair.*

Plate 39 *Detail of Christ and the Virgin.*

Plate 41 *Detail of the Blessed Souls.*

Plate 42 *Detail of the Damned—Charon's boat.*

Plates 43 and **44** *The Conversion of Saul. The Crucifixion of St Peter.*
Frescoes. Each 20 ft. 6 in. × 21 ft. 8 in. (625 × 661 cm.). Pauline Chapel, Vatican, Rome. 1542–50.
The Pauline Chapel was the private chapel of Pope Paul III, who commissioned the frescoes. The contract was made in October 1541. The *Conversion of Saul* was started late in 1542 and finished in mid-1545; the *Crucifixion of St Peter* was started in March 1546 and finished early in 1550. The combination of these two subjects is unusual: normally the Conversion of Saul was paired with the Presentation of the Keys and the Crucifixion of St Peter with St Paul's Martyrdom.

The choice—another instance of the remarkable freedom allowed to Michelangelo by his patrons—clearly has strong autobiographical significance. It was followed by Caravaggio in his two altarpieces for Santa Maria del Popolo (1600–1).

Plates 45 and **46** *The Piazza del Campidoglio,* Capitoline Hill, Rome. About 1539/46–1564. (See also figure 7.)
The contract for this commission is lost. Ackerman believes that Michelangelo was working on it as early as 1539, but it is unlikely that he was actually commissioned as the architect until 1546, the year when Sangallo, the Pope's architect, died. His earliest contribution was the base (1538–39) for the Marcus Aurelius monument, which was brought to the site in 1538.

The Palazzo del Senatore and the Palazzo dei Conservatori (plate 46) already existed: Michelangelo dressed them with a façade one bay deep. He exploited their irregular relationship by designing a third palace, called the 'Palazzo Nuovo', which was not required by the contract, to match the Conservatori (figure 7).

By the time of his death a substantial start to the work on the Senatore and Conservatori Palaces had been made. Giacomo della Porta (appointed 1564) supervised their completion. The central bay of the Conservatori is his new design. Of the existing Senatore façade, only the staircase (about 1547–52) is original: Michelangelo's campanile was destroyed by lightning in 1577 and the whole façade was reduced in magnificence by della Porta's new designs, which were finished by 1612. The third palace was built 1602–54 as an exact replica of the Conservatori.

The pavement was reconstructed in 1940 from Michelangelo's design (figure 7). Some of the subtlety of his plan was lost in introducing four exits into the shallow steps. The triangular relationship of the three original exits was obviously intended as a foil to the placing of the three palaces.

The Capitoline Hill was known as the site of ancient Roman temples and overlooks the Forum. As well as the Marcus Aurelius, the square was also decorated with the antique Castor and Pollux flanking the ramp and the River Gods in the Senatore staircase. Other antique pieces have since been removed into the museum of the Conservatori. Several inscriptions in the piazza refer to the parallel between ancient and modern Rome.

Plate 47 *The Porta Pia, Rome. 1561–64.*
The contract was made on July 2nd, 1561, for a city gate to complete the new Via Pia, conceived by Pope Pius IV in his own honour. City gates of the period were almost expected to be eccentric. Michelangelo's invention was concentrated on the central porch, whose rich forms are contrasted with the flat simplicity elsewhere (as the tombs are with the upper storeys of the Medici Chapel). The existing structure, although unfinished at his death, is faithful to his design with two exceptions. An engraving of 1568 shows his intention to raise an obelisk topped by a sphere at each end of the façade. The crowning Baroque pediment was added by Vespignani in 1853 after damage by lightning.

Plate 48 *St Peter's, Rome. 1547–64.* (See also figure 8.)
Michelangelo was reluctant to accept Pope Paul III's invitation to take over the building of St Peter's and only accepted at the papal command. Nevertheless, during his 17 years as *capomaestro* the work proceeded at a pace unparalleled in the preceding half-century.

The building history St Peter's before Michelangelo's appointment on January 1st, 1547, includes the designs and work of Bramante (1506–14), Raphael (1514–20), Peruzzi (1520–34) and Antonio da Sangallo (1534–46). When he took over, the crossing was complete up to the drum and the four arms either built (two were actually vaulted) or irrevocably determined. So although he obtained permission to pull down a part of the Sangallo scheme he despised so much (a strange,

slightly Gothic axial church of which the very expensive model still exists), he was severely restricted. This—as well as the persistent opposition of Sangallo's reactionary followers—must help to explain his great reluctance to accept the commission.

He received payments for a wooden model (lost) in 1547 and for a second wooden model of the drum and dome, 1558–61, which still exists in the Museo Petriano although altered by della Porta.

By his death the drum was virtually complete inside and out and the two transept arms (north and south) were near enough finished to determine the character of the building's external order. It is possible that the change della Porta imposed upon Michelangelo's dome design (it was heightened) reflects Michelangelo's own second thoughts between 1561 and 1564. Apart from his plan (figure 8) we have no reliable indication of his intention for the façade.

The dome was built under della Porta and Fontana 1588–90 and the lantern 1590–93. The nave and façade were designed by Maderna about 1607 and completed by 1615.

Plate 49 *Pietà. Marble. Height 7 ft. 8 in. (234 cm.). Florence Cathedral. About 1547–55.*
Although all three of the late sculptures are called *Pietàs*, this is only strictly a correct description of the Rondanini (plate 51), where two figures only are involved. This work is iconographically a fusion of a Deposition and a Lamentation, and the Palestrina *Pietà* (plate 50) is really an Entombment.

Some of the execution (particularly of the Magdalen) is by his assistant Tiberio Calcagni, after Michelangelo had partially destroyed the unfinished group, apparently frustrated by the imperfect marble. Christ's left leg was made from a separate stone, and not restored, but its position is known through copies.

The group was begun around 1547 and mutilated at some time before December 1555. Vasari says that Michelangelo intended the group for his own tomb and acknowledged the Nicodemus as a self-portrait.

The statue stood in the crypt of San Lorenzo during the seventeenth century; in 1721 was transferred to the Cathedral.

Plate 50 *Pietà. (The Palestrina Pietà.) Marble. Height 8 ft. 2½ in. (205.5 cm.). Accademia, Florence. About 1556.*
Not mentioned by the early sources and first recorded as by

Michelangelo in the eighteenth century, this work is not accepted by several scholars, although in form and content it is closely related to his late works. The dating is suggested first by its clear relationship to a sheet of drawings at Oxford (Ashmolean, Cat. No. 70) which also contains studies for the Rondanini, and secondly by the closeness to the Rondanini itself, where the transcendental quality, only partially developed here, is finally realised.

The block had been previously carved for another purpose—there are traces of architectural ornament—and was probably finished in places (torso of Christ and the Virgin's right hand) by assistants. (See note on plate 49.) First recorded in Santa Rosalia, Palestrina, in the seventeenth century, hence the name.

Plates 51 and **52** *Pietà*. (The Rondanini Pietà.) Marble. Height 6 ft. 3⅝ in. (190.5 cm.). Castello Sforzesco, Milan. About 1552–64.
The first version (of which the disembodied right arm of Christ still remains) was probably started about 1552, and the complete reworking begun after the partial destruction of the Florentine *Pietà*. Michelangelo was seen by Daniele da Volterra working on this sculpture six days before his death. It acquired its name because during the nineteenth century it stood in the Palazzo Rondanini in Rome. Acquired by the City of Milan in 1952.

Plate 53 *Deposition*. Red chalk. 14¾ in. × 11 in. (37.5 × 28 cm.). Ashmolean Museum, Oxford. Cat. No. 37. About 1555.
This is one of the most dramatic drawings of this and related subjects that Michelangelo executed in the 1550s. Its authenticity has been doubted by some scholars but it is accepted by Johannes Wilde, the most reliable authority on the drawings. (See note on figure 9.)

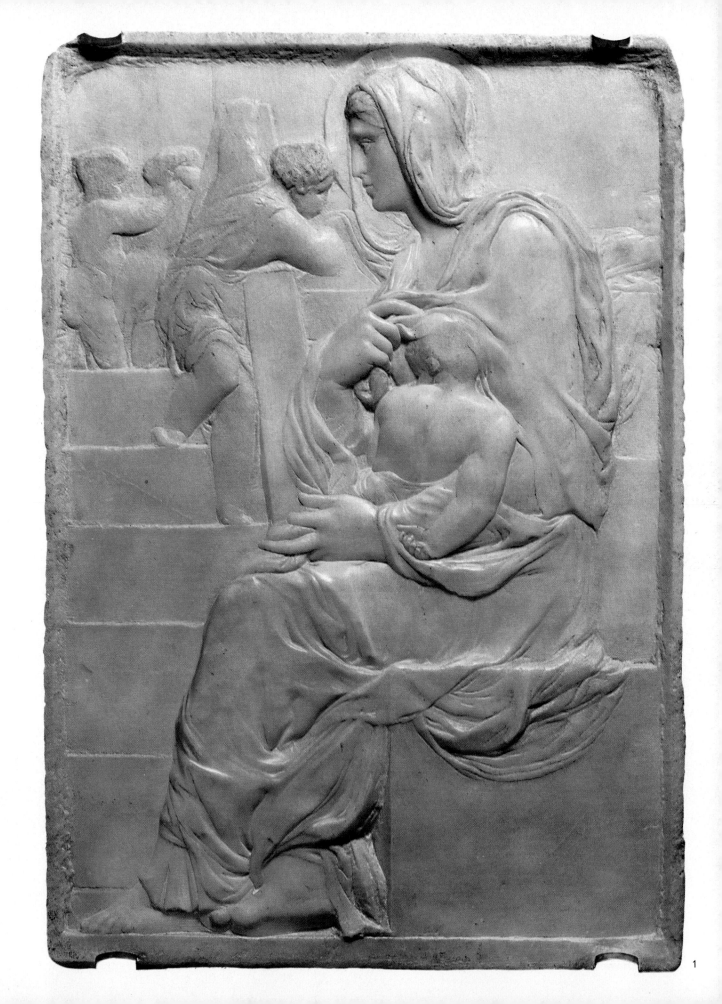

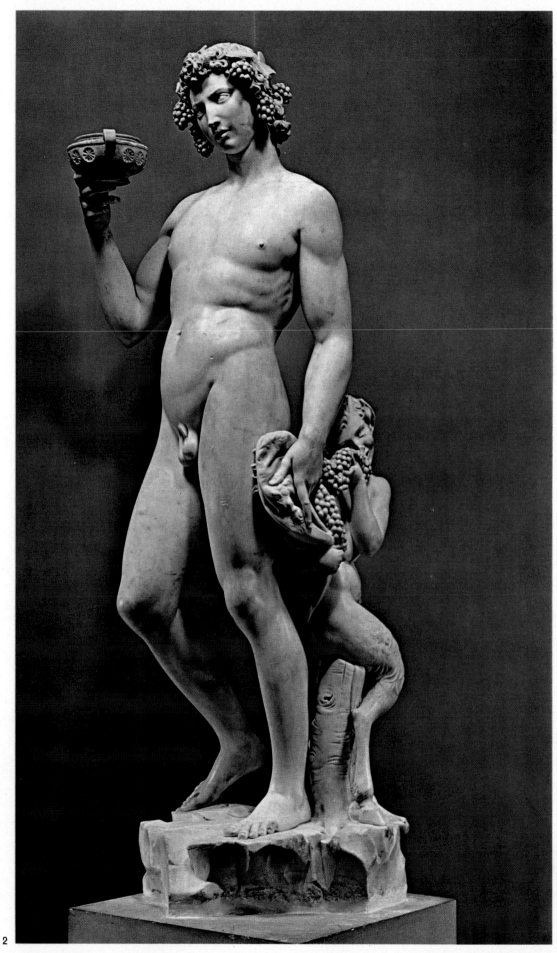

2

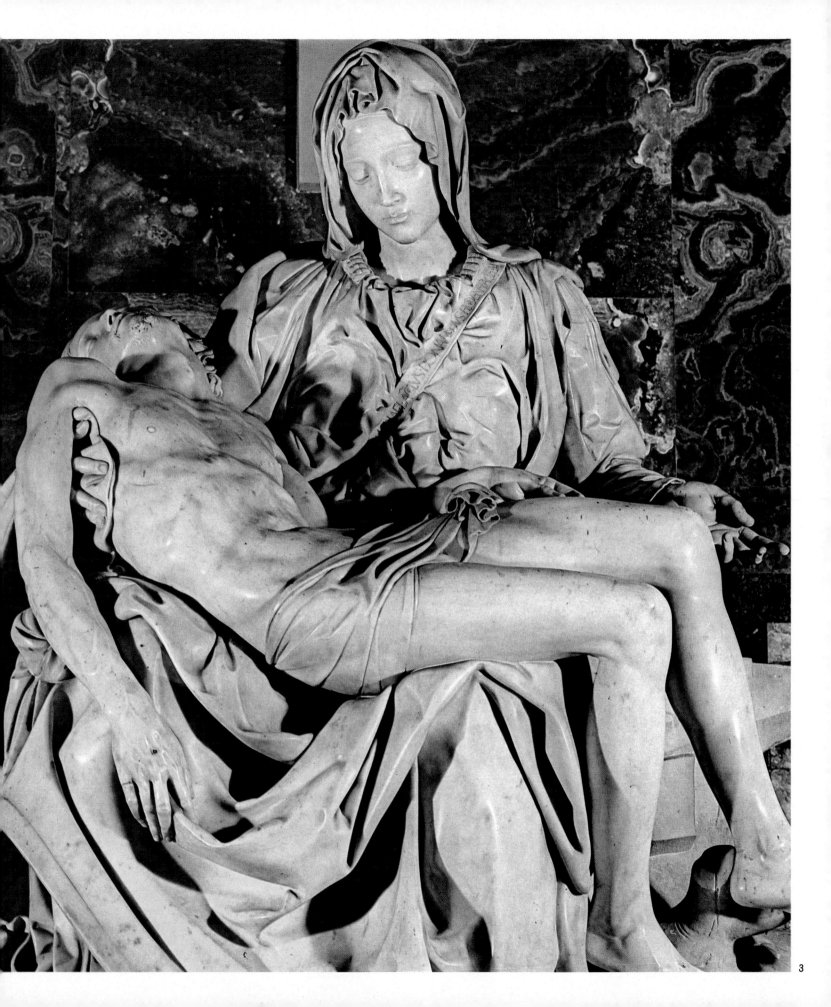

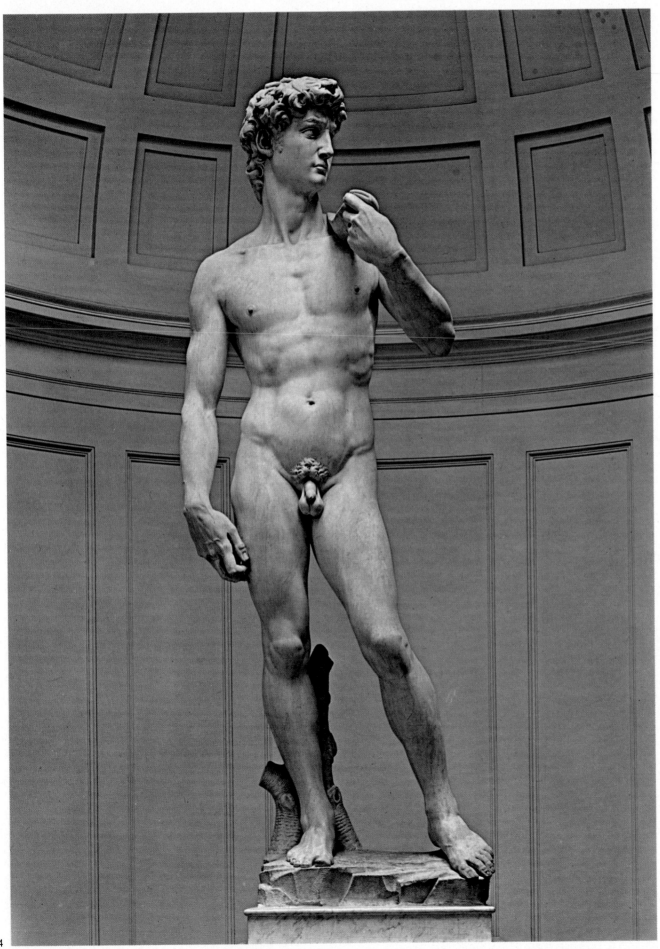

4

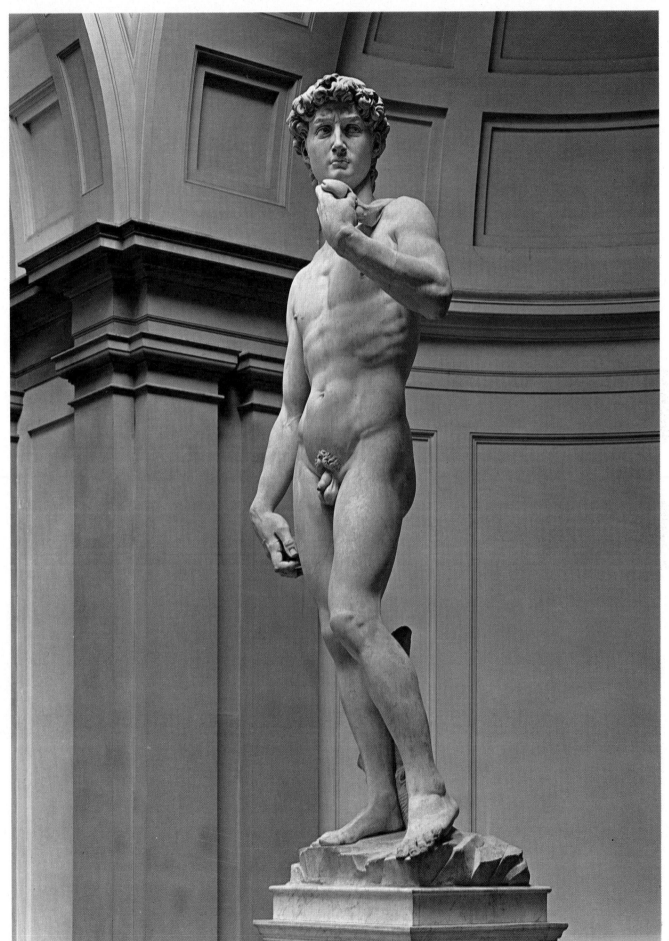

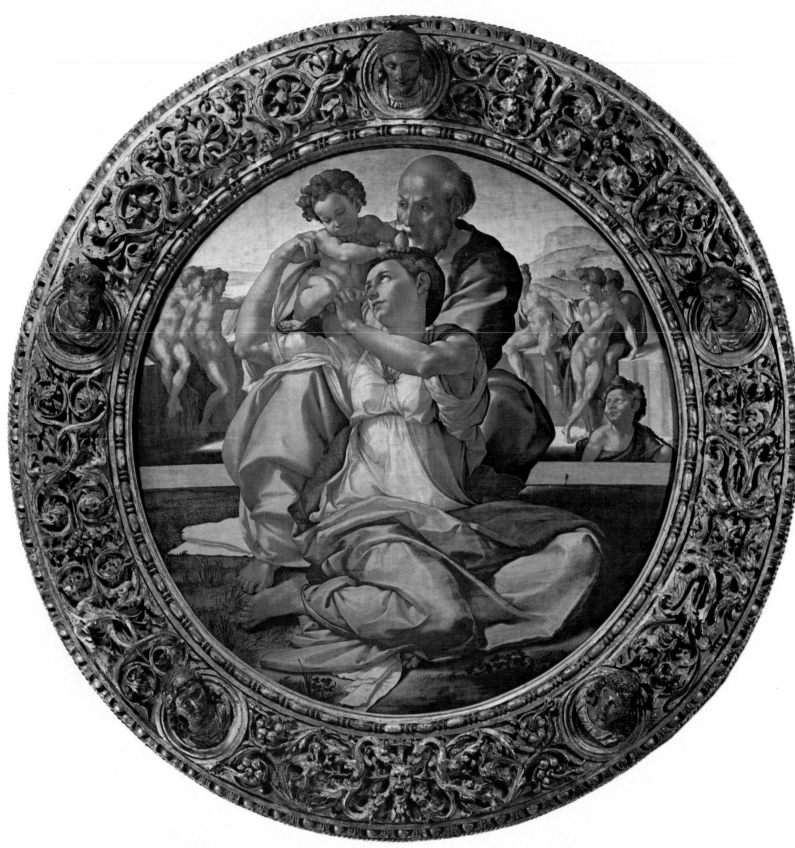

6

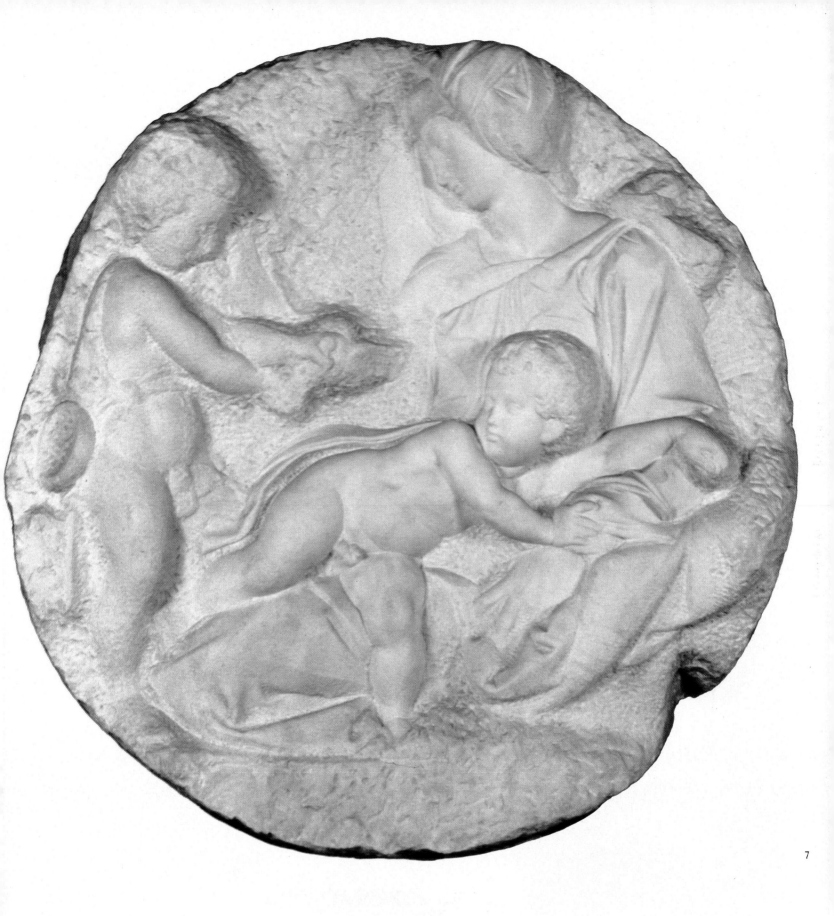

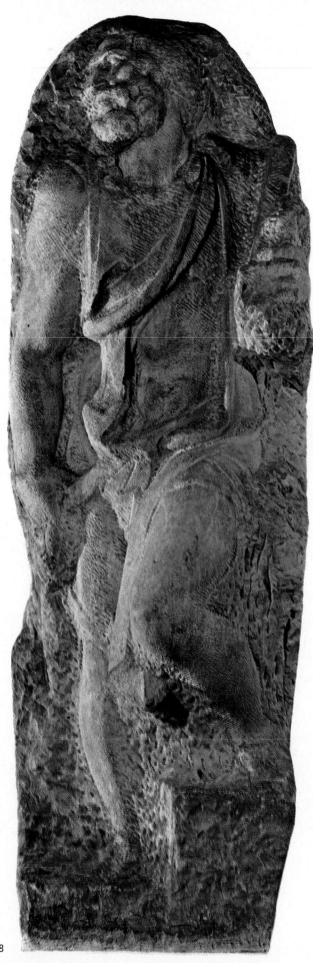

8

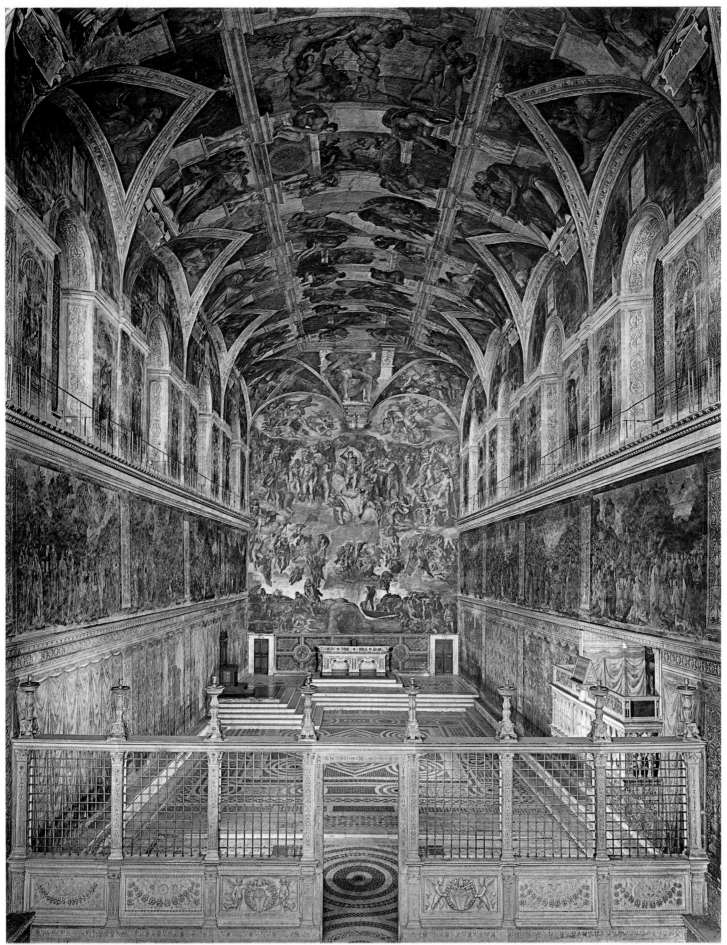

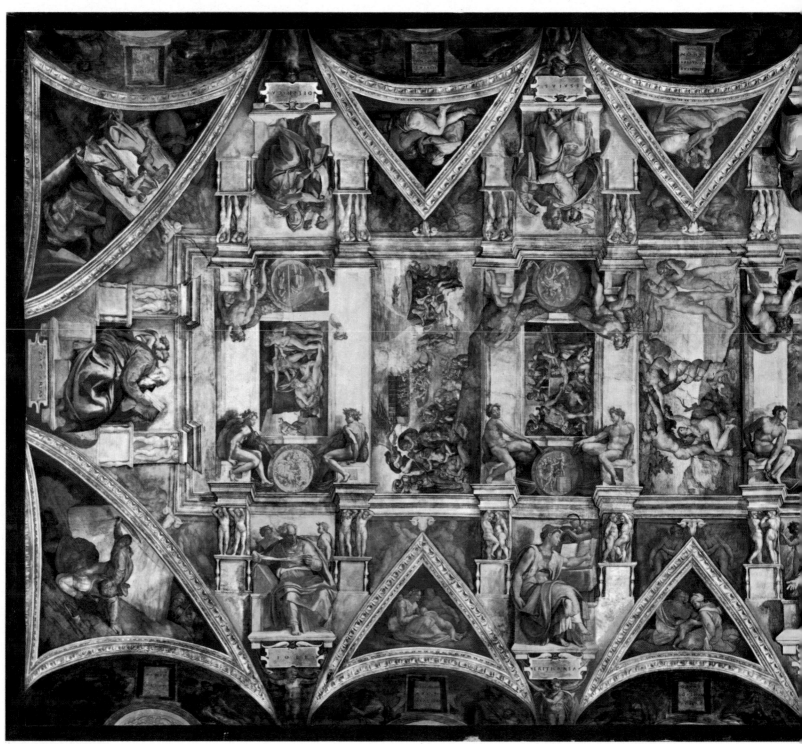

10

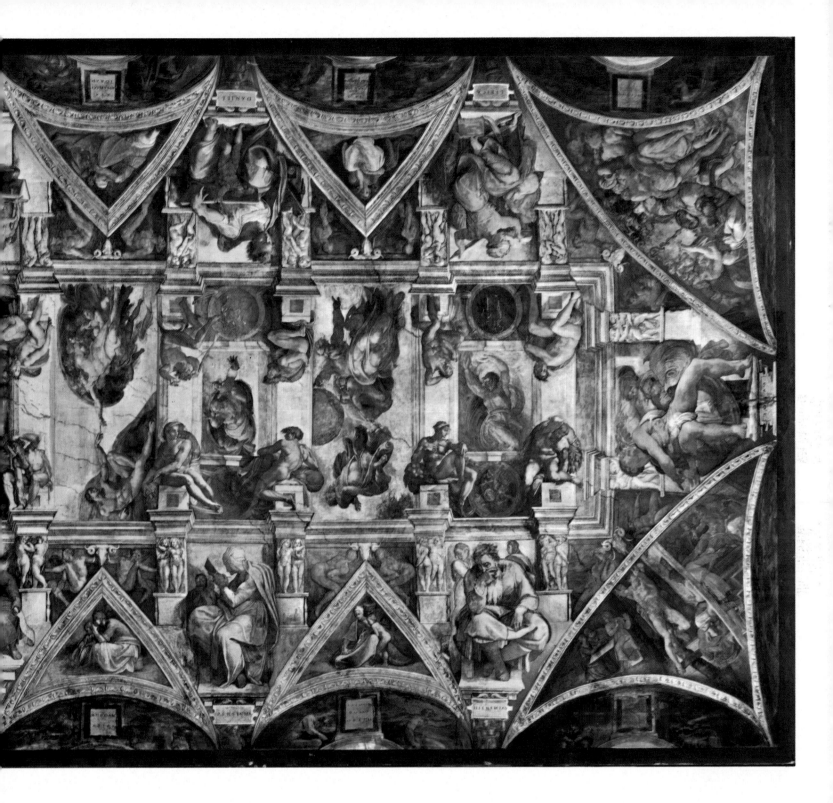

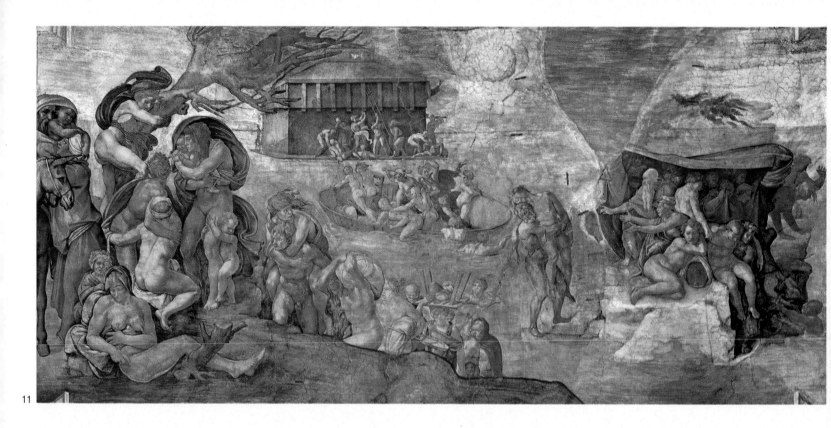

11

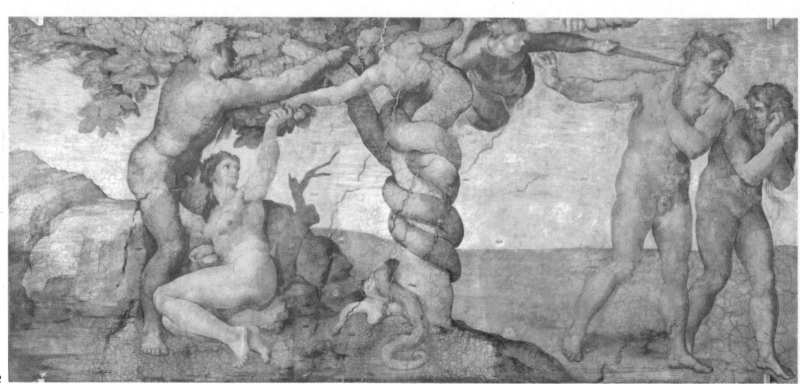

12

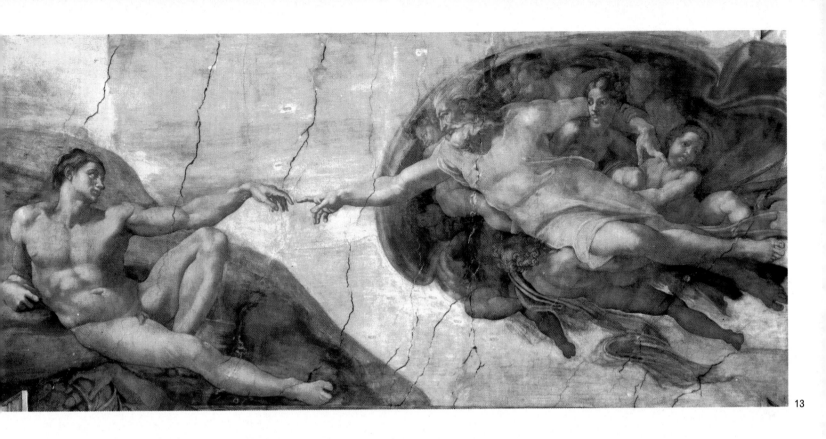

13

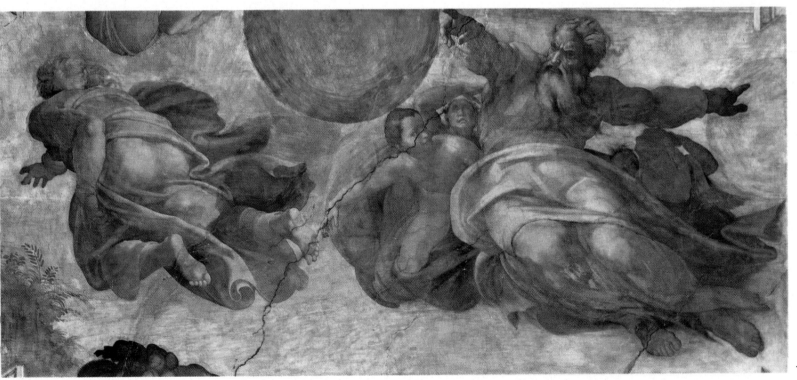

14

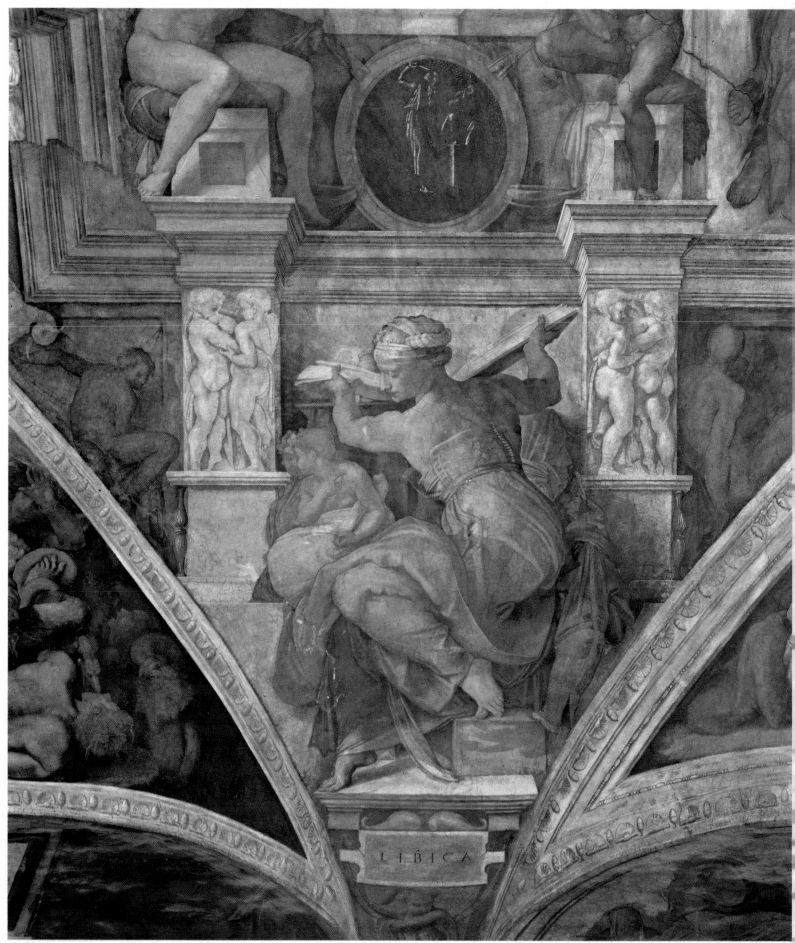

LIBICA

15

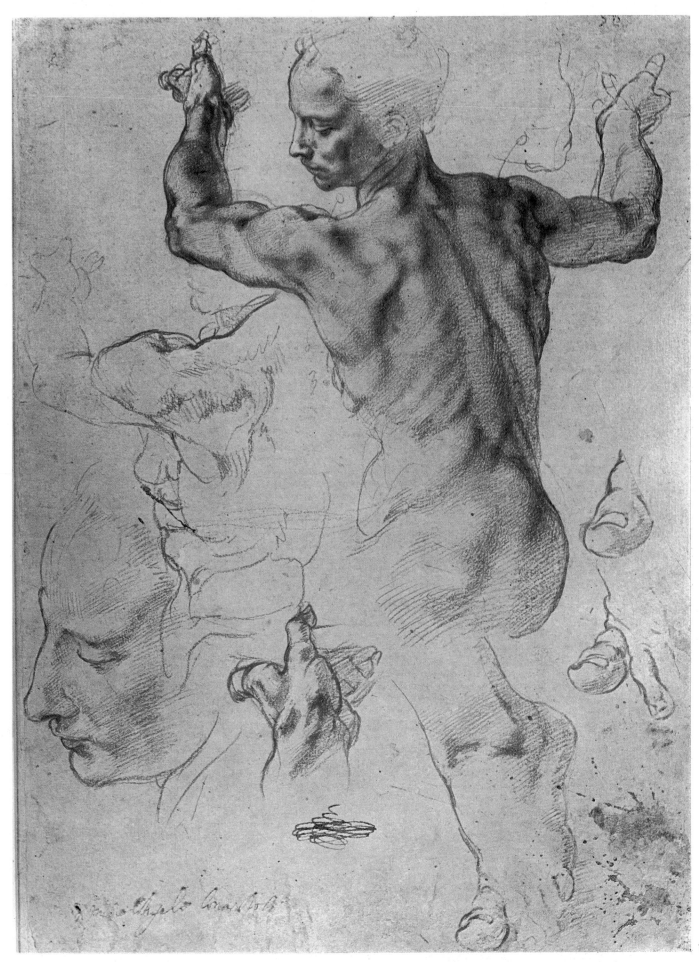

16

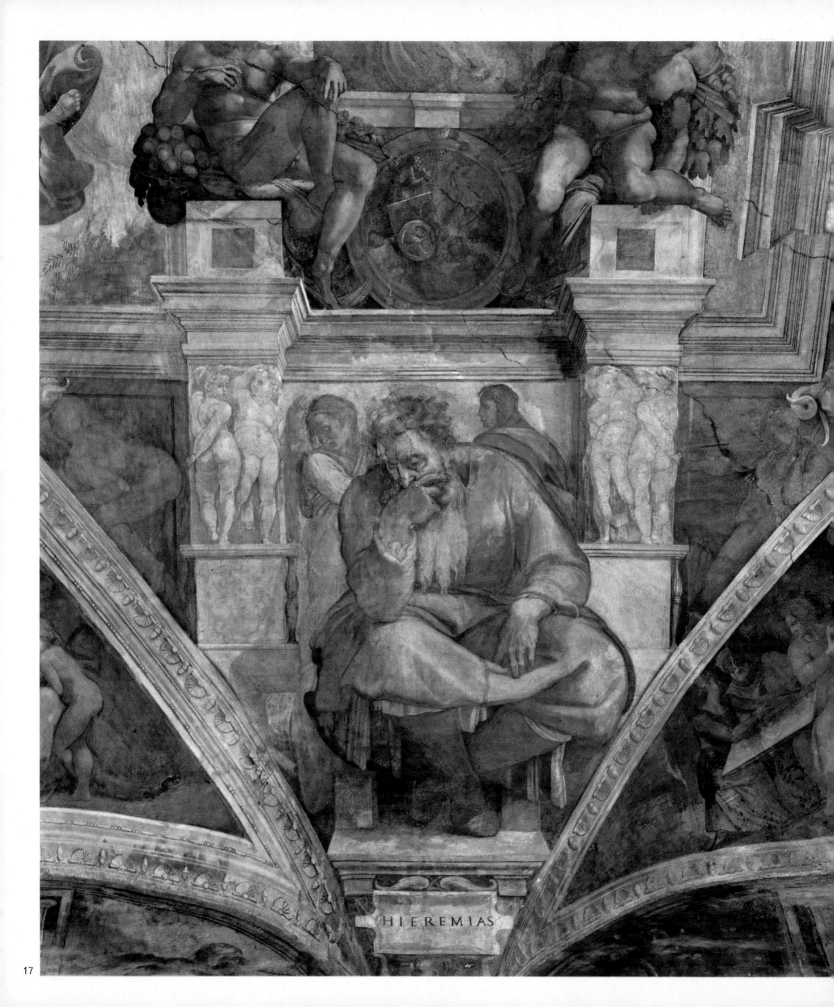

HIEREMIAS

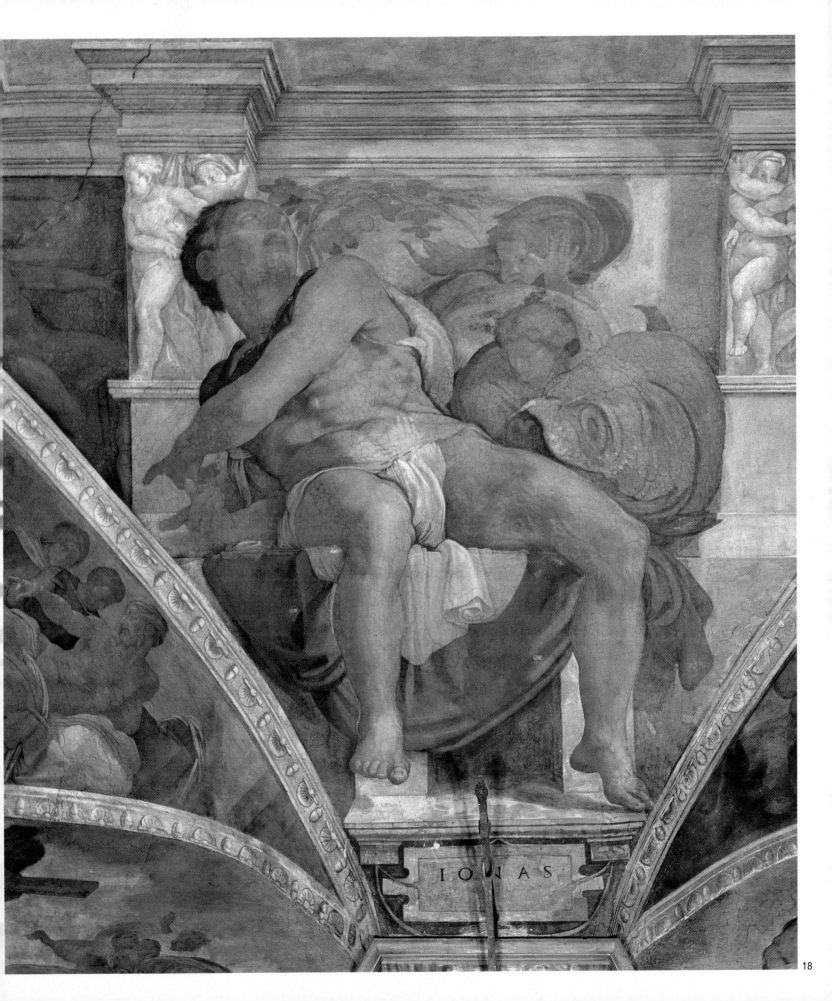

IO᱘AS

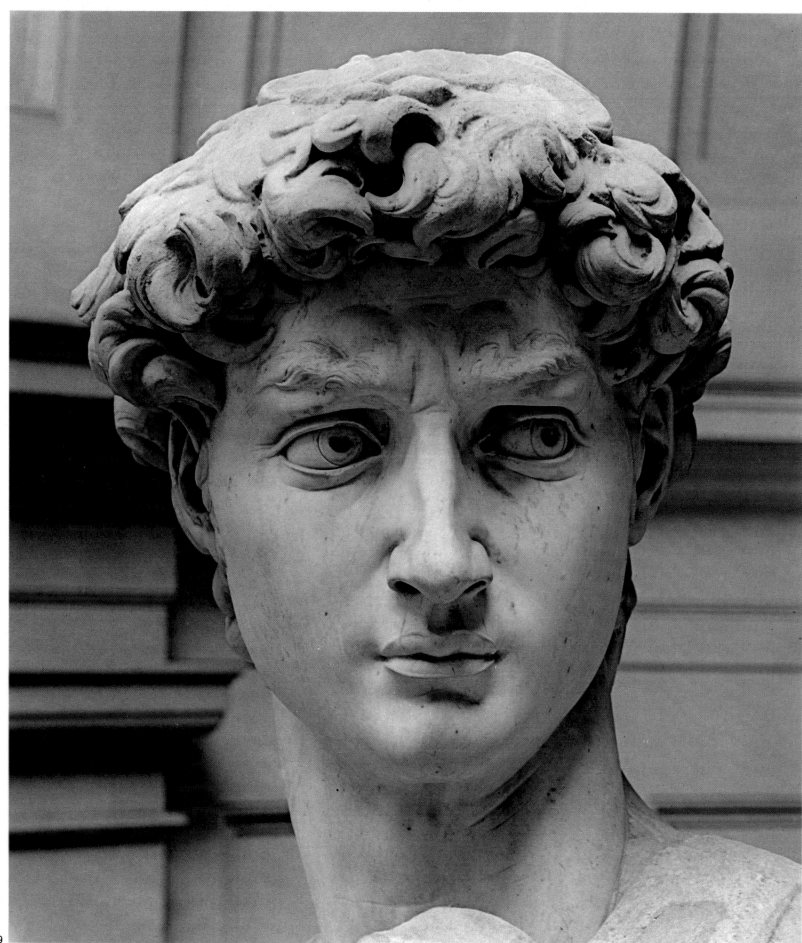

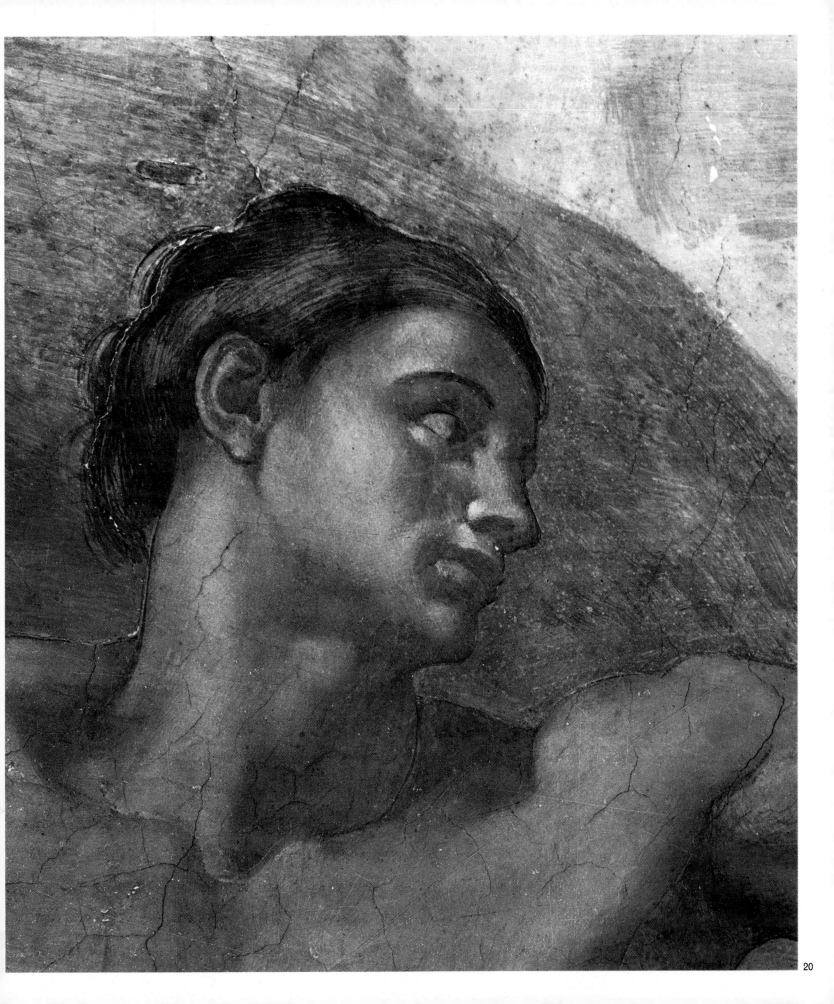

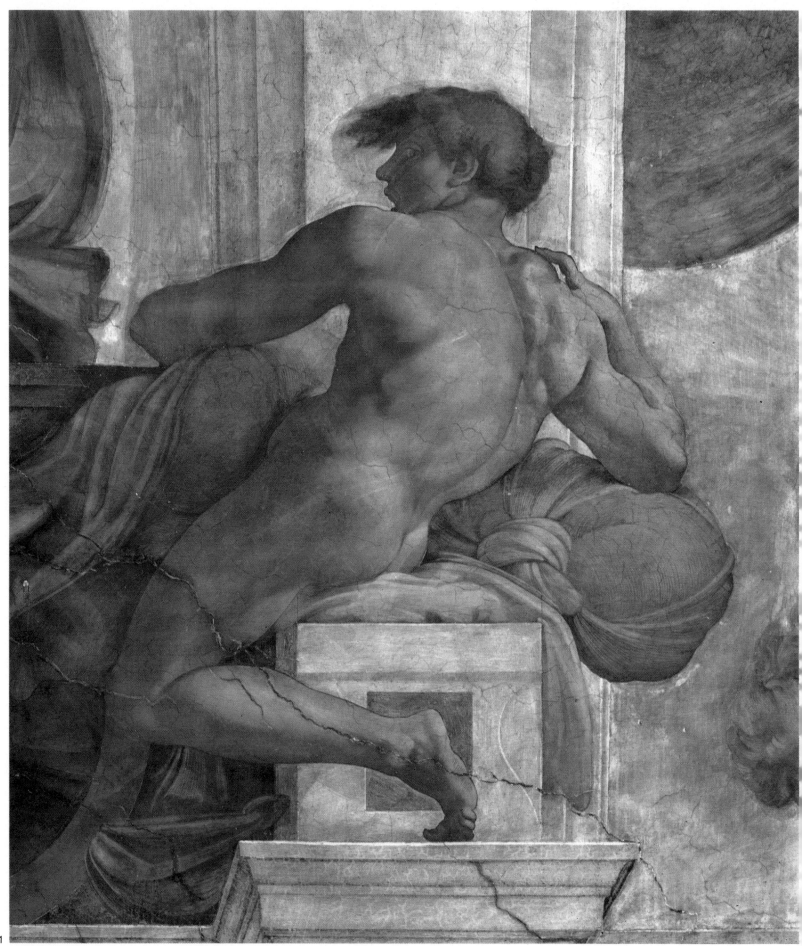

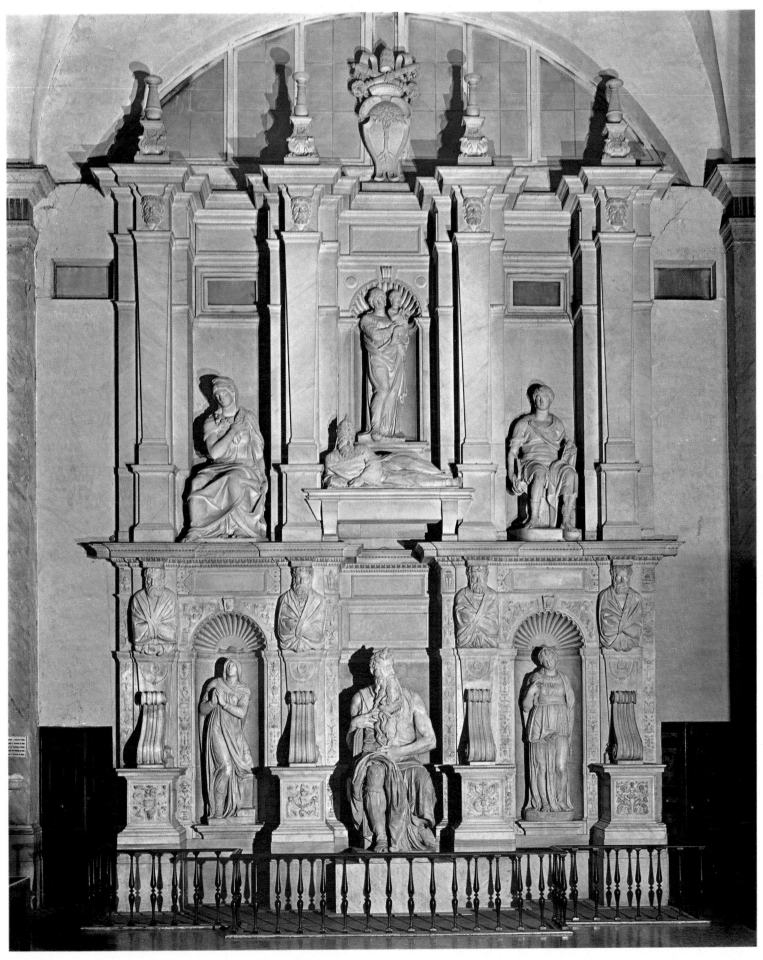

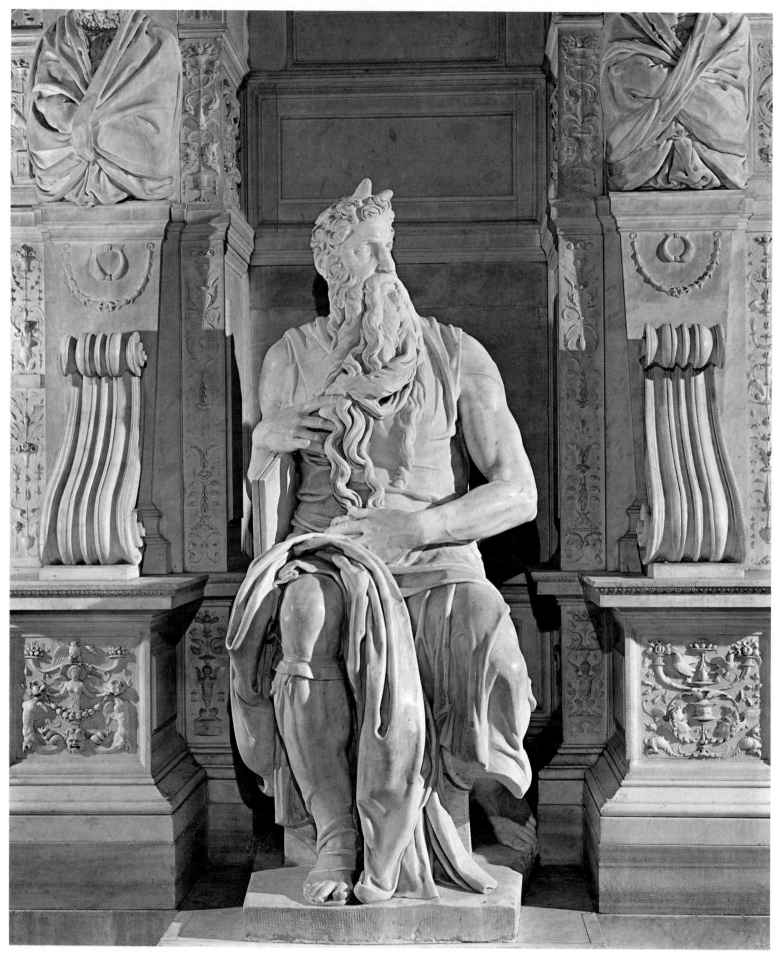

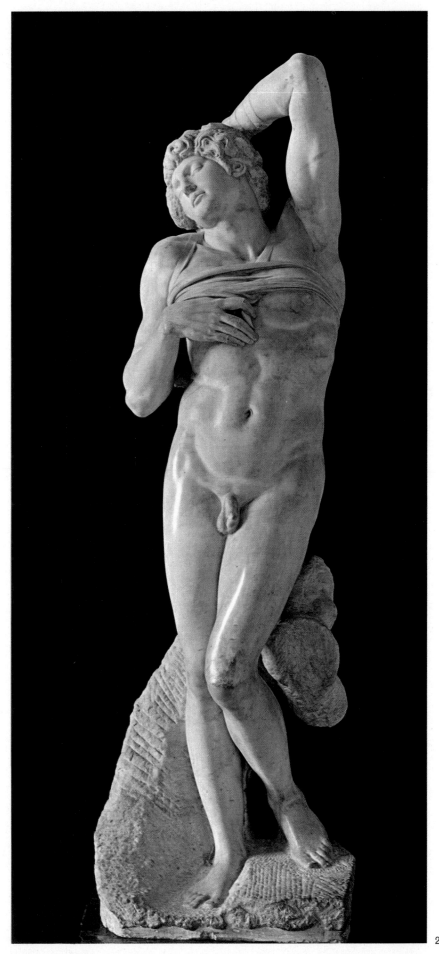

24

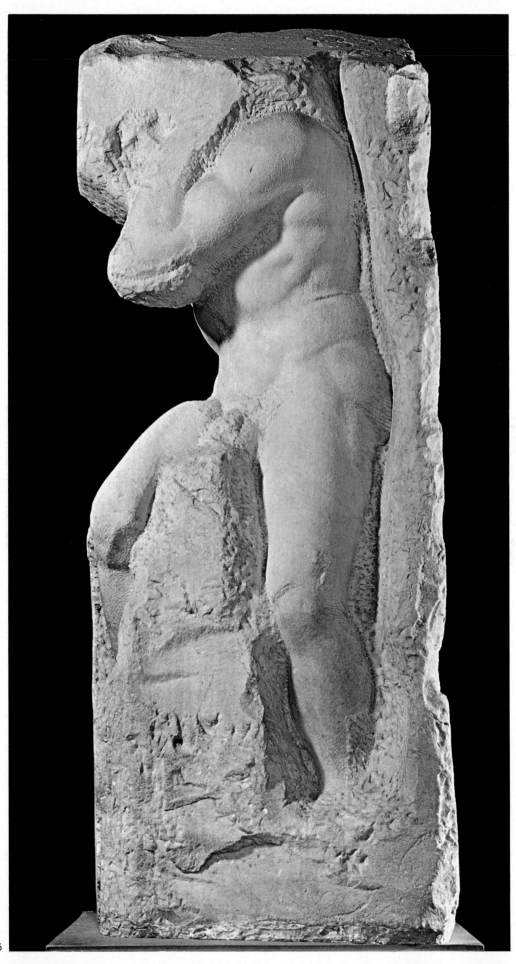

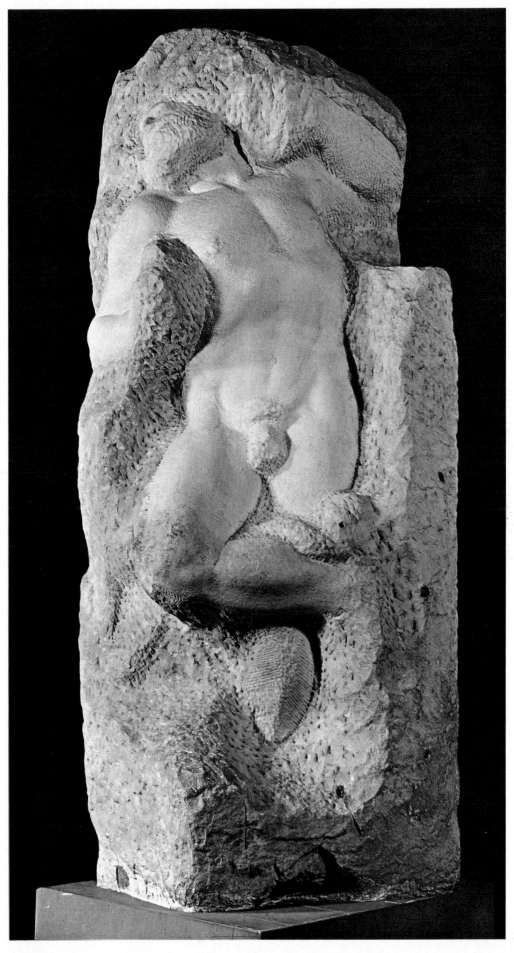

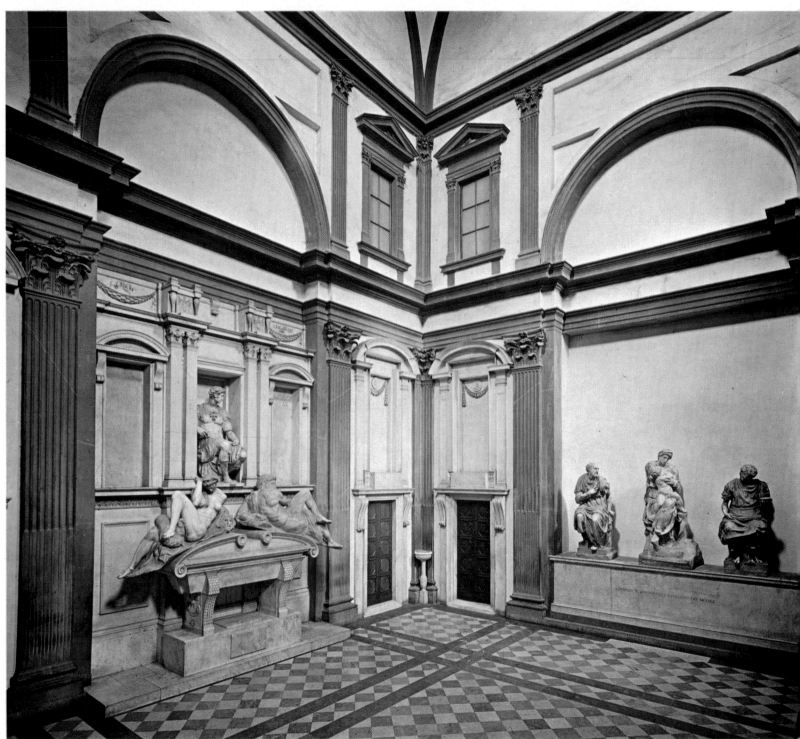

27

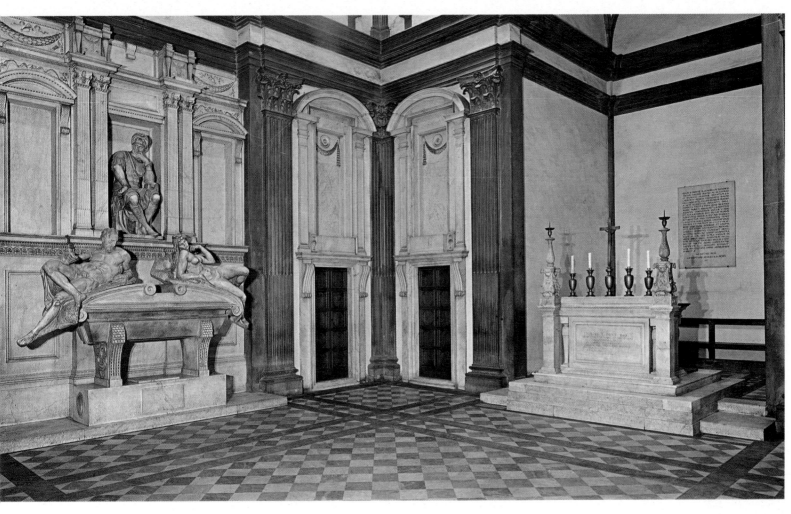

28

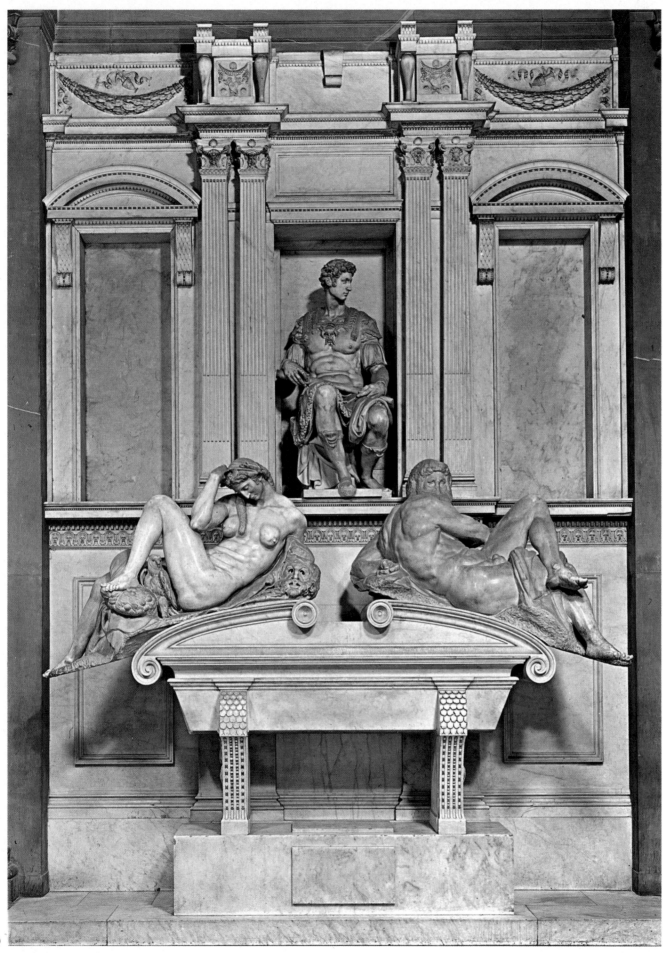

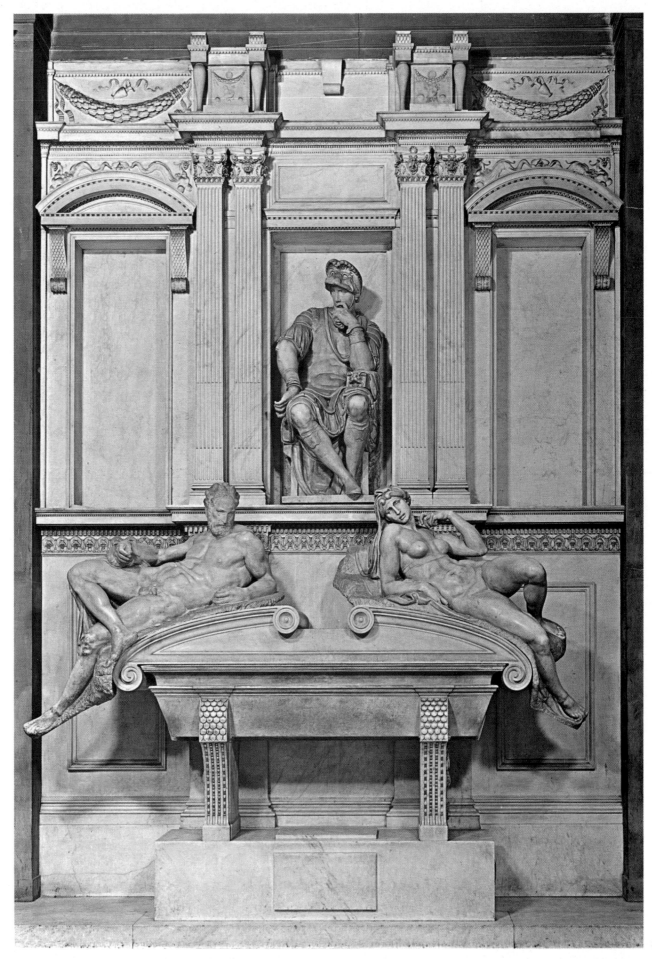

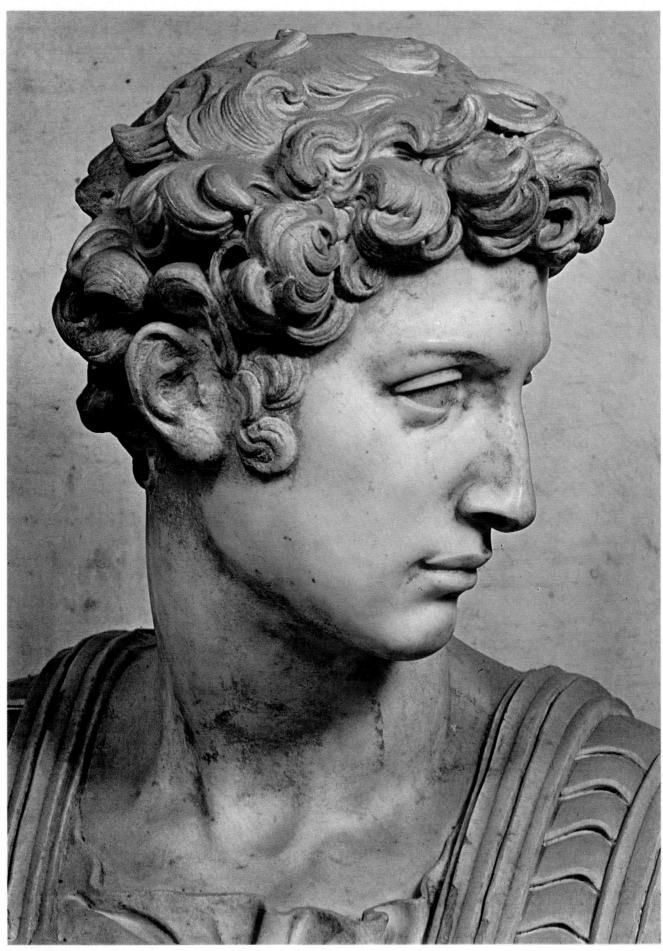

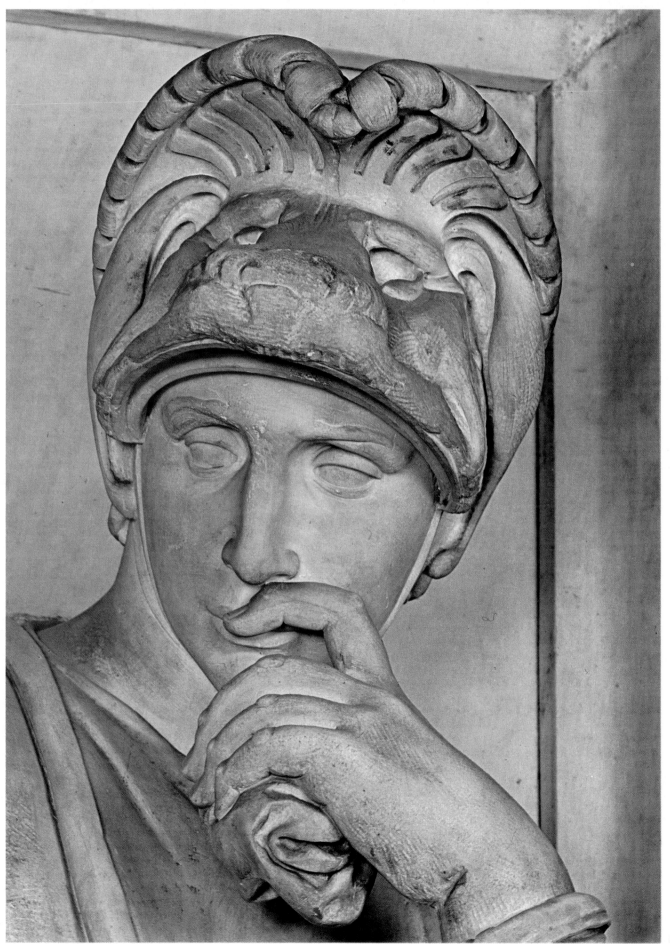

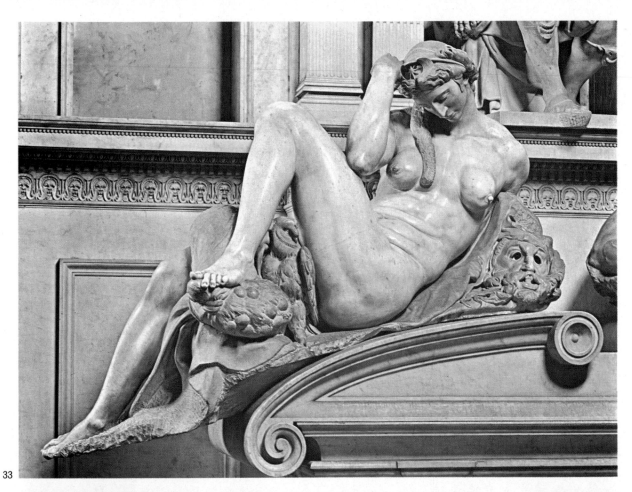

33

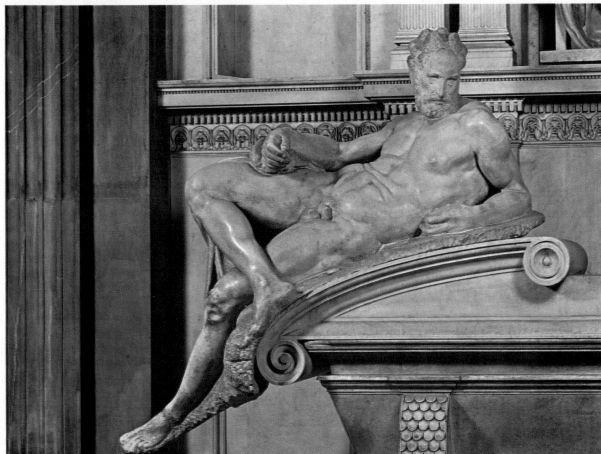

34

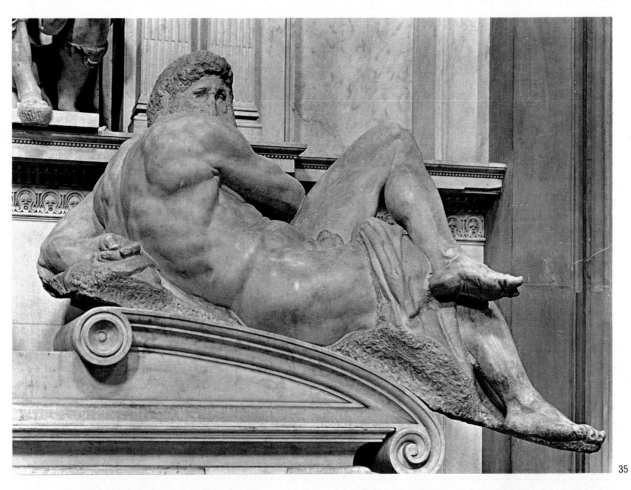

35

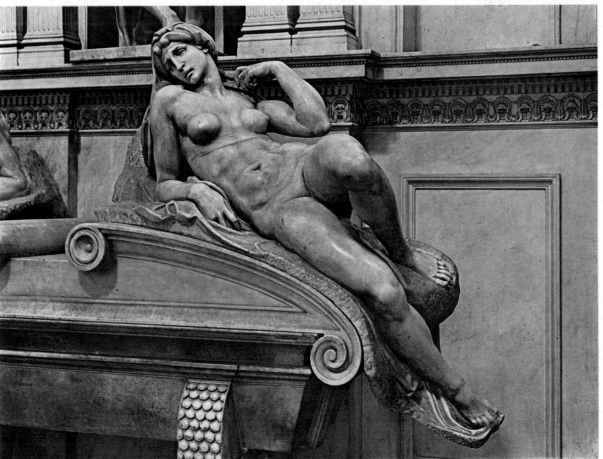

36

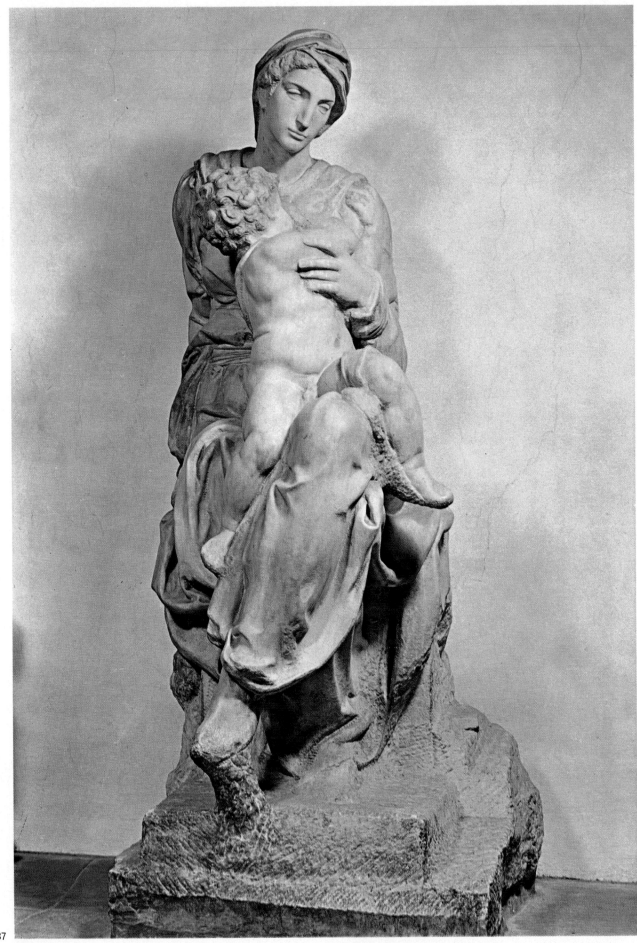

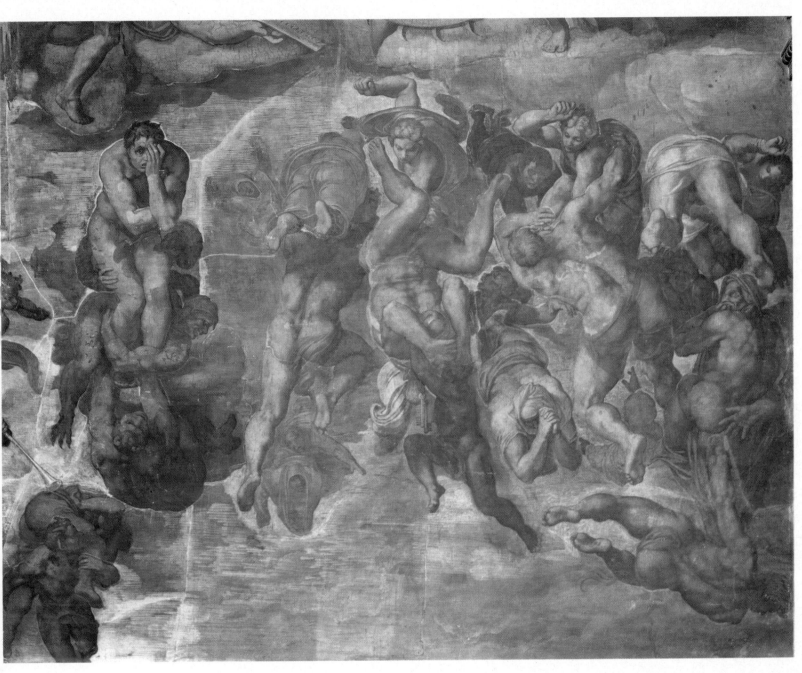

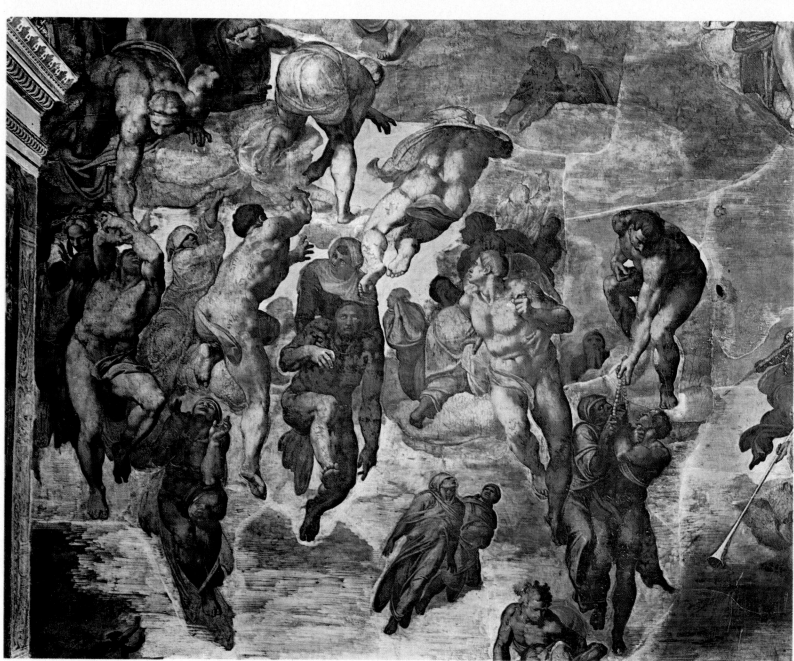

41

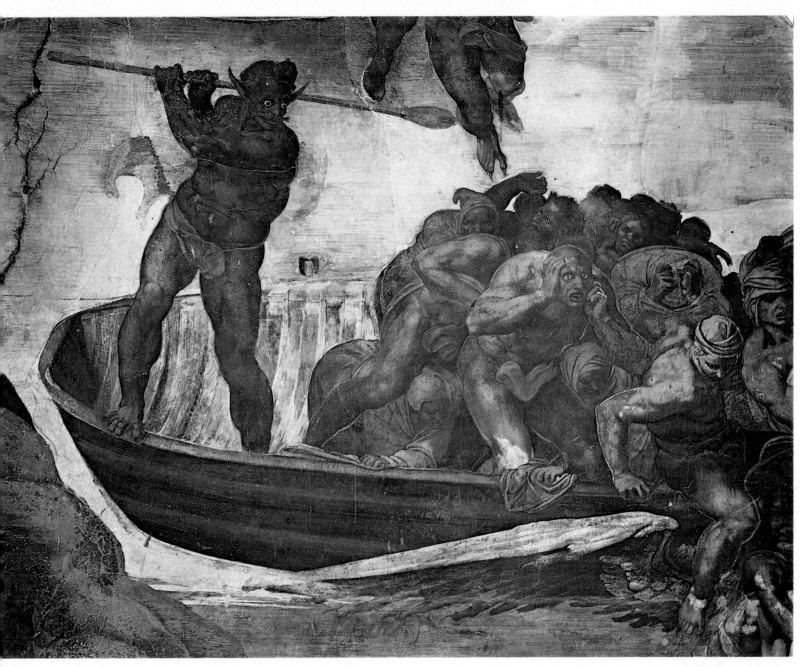

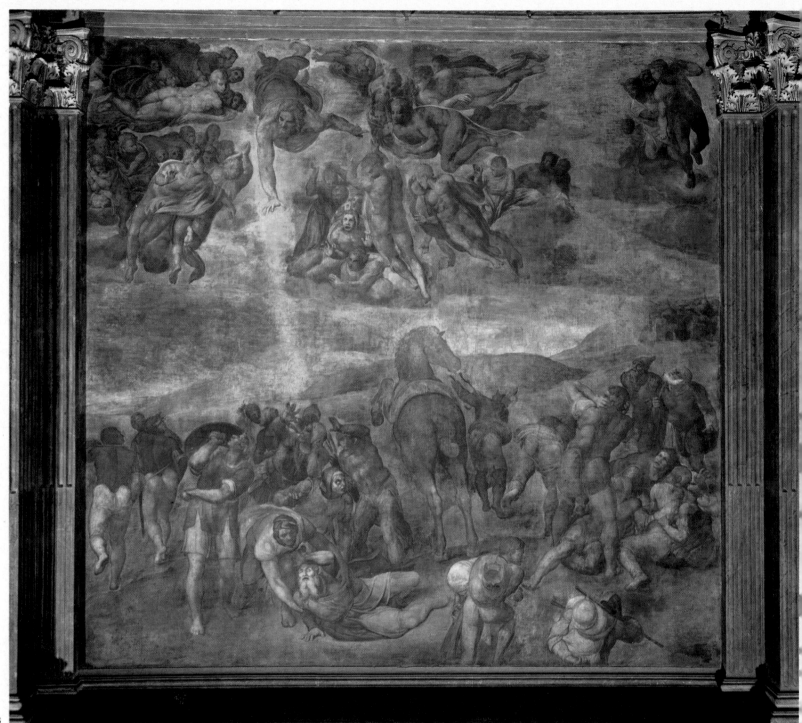

43

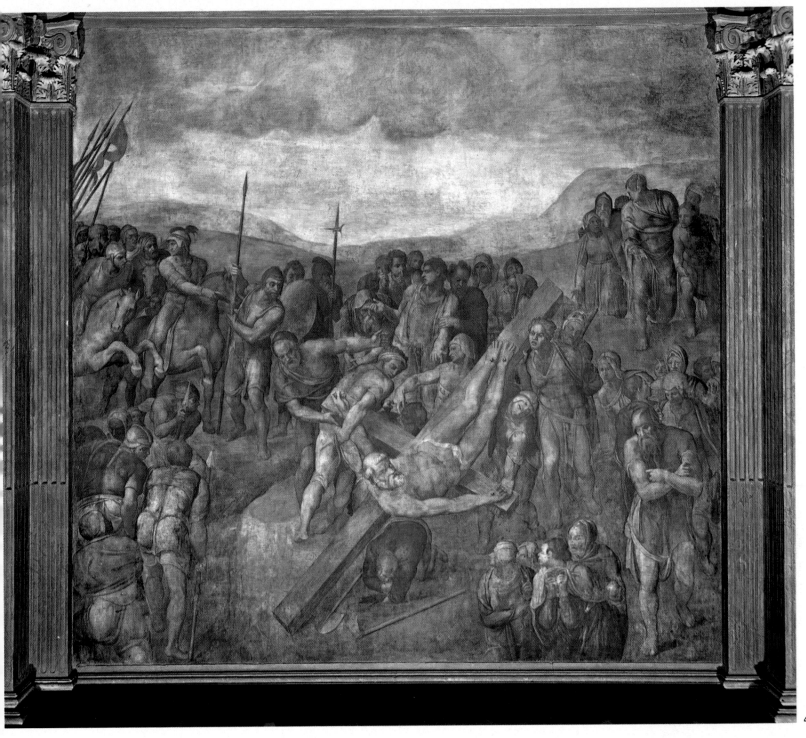

44

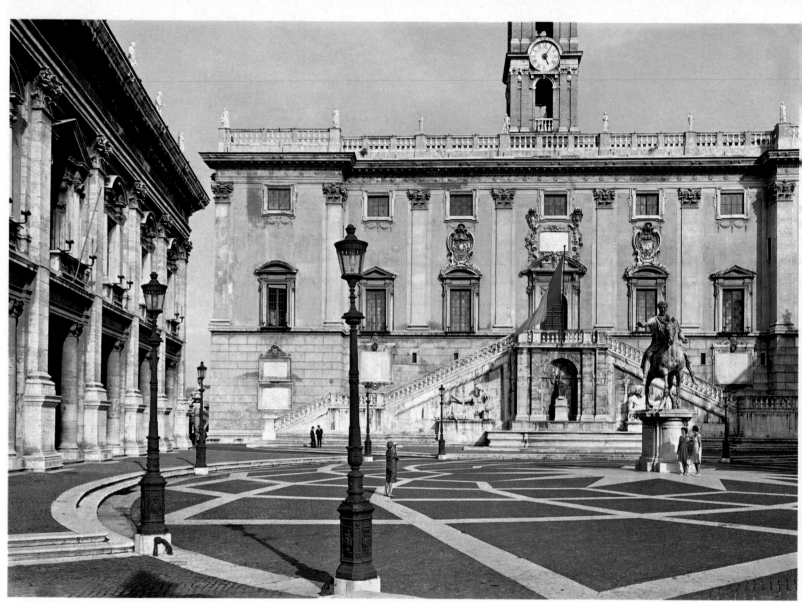

45

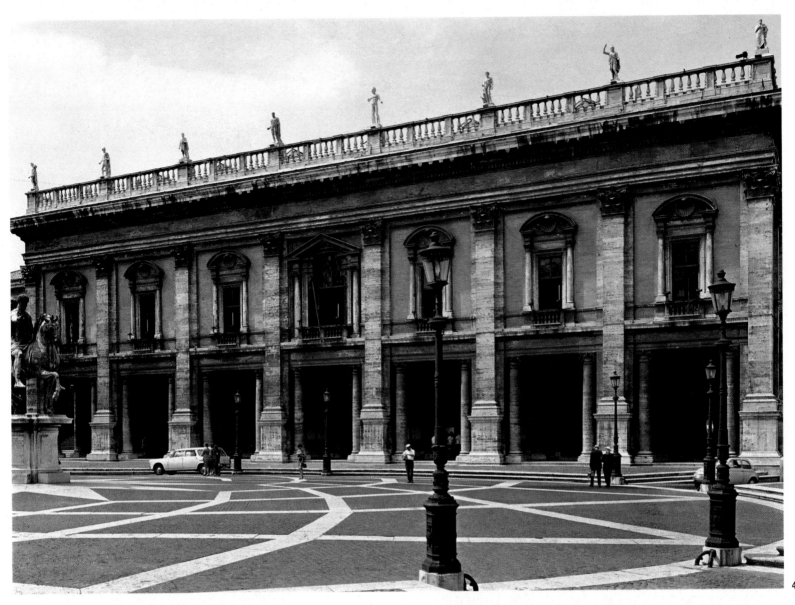

46

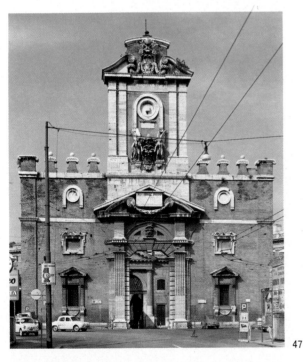

47

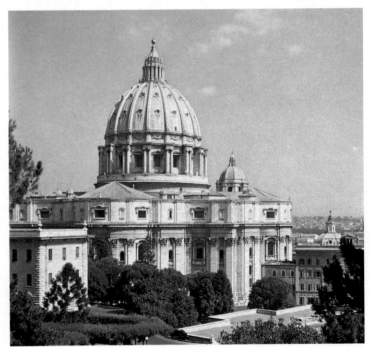

48

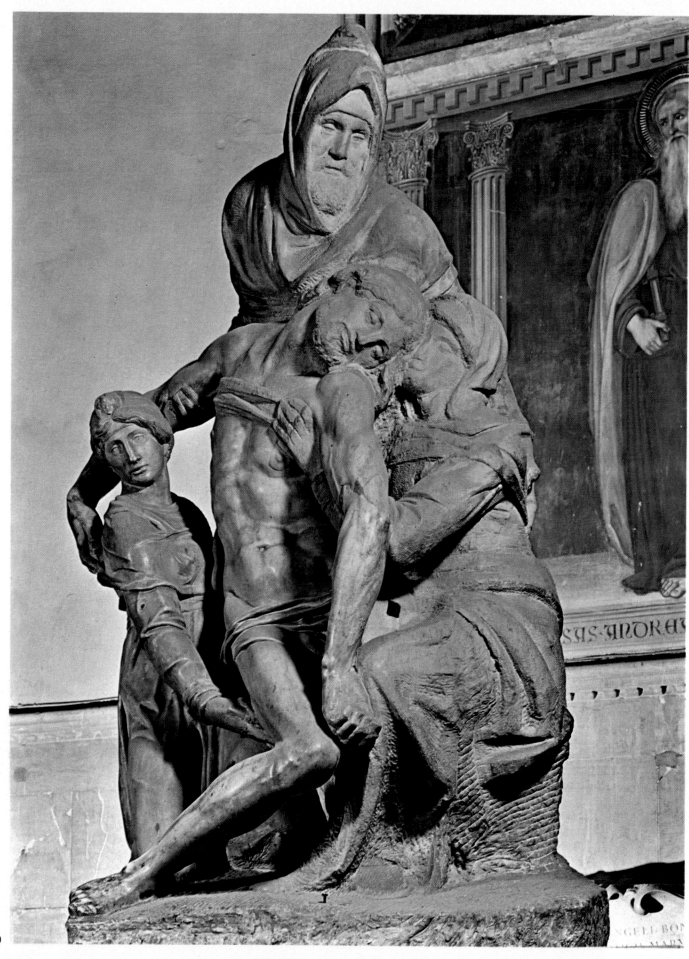

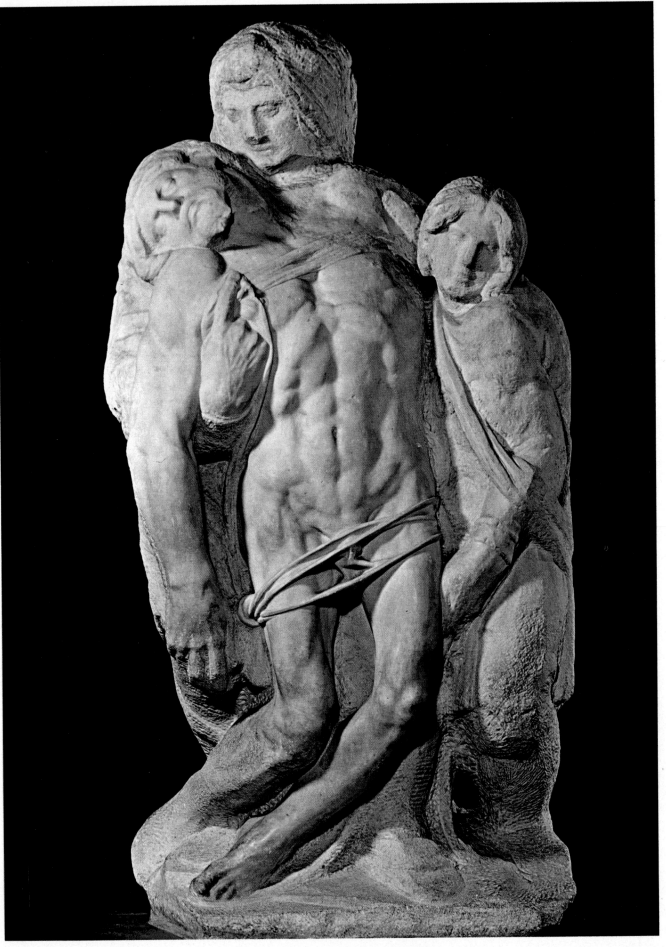

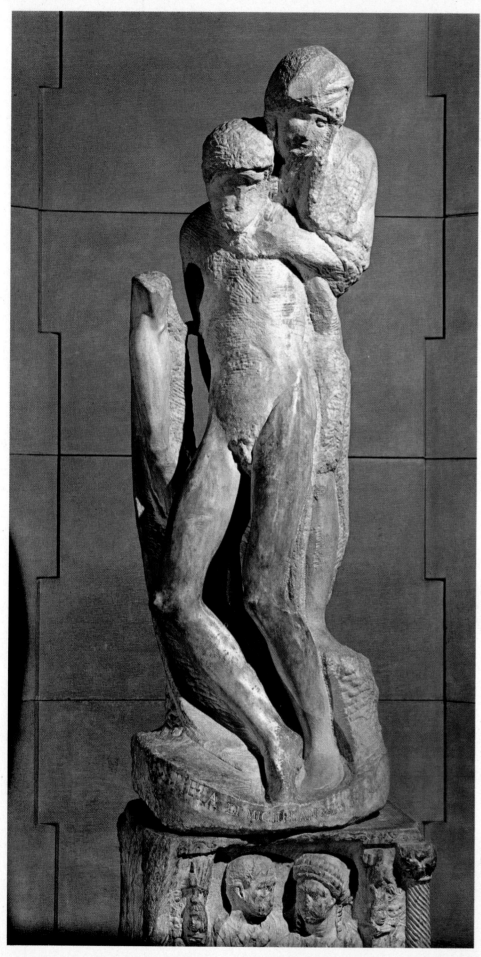

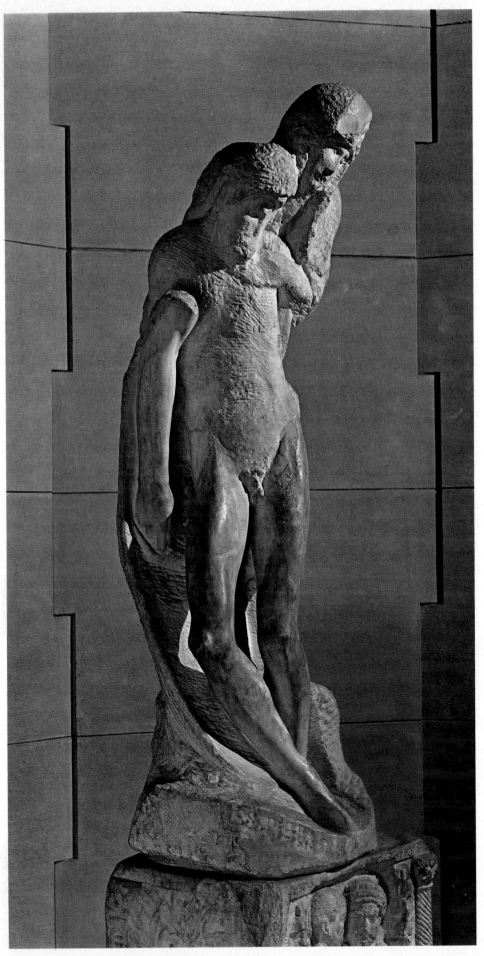

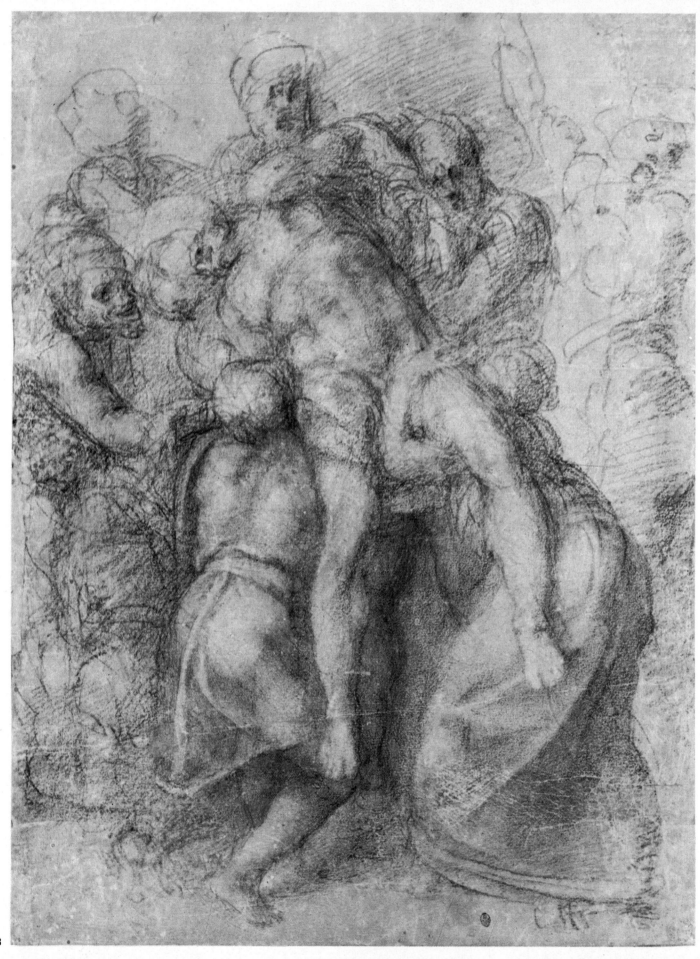

53